A SPIRITUAL CLINIC

A Suggestive Diagnosis and Prescription
for
Problems in Christian Life
and Service

By
J. OSWALD SANDERS

MOODY PRESS
CHICAGO

ISBN 0-8024-0070-1

2 3 4 5 6 7 Printing/LC/Year 87 86 85 84 83 82

Printed in the United States of America

INTRODUCTION

THE PRIMARY OBJECTIVE of this book is indicated in its title. Its thesis is that complex
strains and problems which the Christian worker
encounters in the contemporary world find their
answer, not in tranquilizers or stimulants, but in
a correct understanding and application of scriptural principles, and effectiveness in Christian work
is the natural outcome of conformity to spiritual
laws enunciated in the Scriptures.

The method of treatment varies. In some cases
the problem and its suggested solution are il-
lustrated by a Bible character or incident. In others
the answer is found in the exposition of a Scripture
paragraph, or in the elucidation of scriptural principles. However, in the final analysis there is but
one basic solution—a correct relationship with the
Triune God, who is adequate for every emergency
and competent to deal with the intricacies of every
heart.

If due credit has not been given in any instance,
forbearance is requested as most of these chapters
have been written in travel, when source material
has not been accessible.

—J. OSWALD SANDERS

CONTENTS

PART ONE

PROBLEMS OF CHRISTIAN EXPERIENCE

1

OVERCOMING TENSION
AND STRAIN

I will give you rest.—Matthew 11:28

STRAIN AND TENSION characterize our age. People in all walks of life are subject to their ravages, and if the truth be told, despite the rich promises of heart-rest and serenity held out to the believing soul, Christians are too readily subject to these same disorders. Even ministers and missionaries, who by common consent are expected to know more of God and His ways than the rank and file of Christians, are by no means exempt from harmful nervous tension. In spite of tears and prayers and self-reproach there are some who seem unable to enter into the rest that remains to the people of God. This should not and need not be.

During the earlier years of his missionary career, and for several years after his founding of the China Inland Mission, Dr. J. Hudson Taylor had been in this plight. Then came his transforming experience. "He had been a toiling, burdened man before, with latterly not much rest of soul," one wrote of him at that time. Then came a fresh meeting with God, a fresh discovery of His endless resources which resulted in a radically changed testimony. "As to work, mine was never so plentiful, so responsible or so difficult, *but the weight and strain are all gone.*" Since God is not guilty of favoritism, we can expect that what He has done for one of His children He is willing to do for all.

The word *tension* is defined as "the state of being strained to stiffness; hence mental strain, intensity of striving, nervous anxiety with attending muscular tenseness." It is, of course, not suggested that all nervous tension is harmful. The string of a harp fulfills its function only as it attains the tension necessary to produce the correct musical note. And so it is with the human life. Its highest achievement is reached only when every power is harnessed to the fulfillment of a worthy life purpose, and this involves a certain degree of tension. One rendering of the words of our Lord in Luke 12:50 is, "What tension I suffer until it is all over!" The fulfillment of the will of God involved Him in tension.

Strain is defined as "excessive tension," and it is with strains and tensions that are harmful and unnecessary that we are concerned.

CONTRIBUTORY CAUSES

A common misconception is that it is hard work which generates tension, but work *per se* is not the real cause. Work, even hard work, when the mind is at rest, is health giving. It produces fatigue but not tension. The fundamental cause of strain is to be found in the mind, not in the body. There would appear to be at least four factors which induce a condition of strain in the Christian worker.

A sense of inadequacy, a haunting conciousness of the lack of spiritual resources and mental acumen for the ministry entrusted to one is a prolific source of tension for it is usually so well based. Which of us *is* adequate for his spiritual ministry? Would not a sense of complete adequacy be proof of our spiritual inadequacy? But with this conscious deficiency, the more conscientious we are the more we strain and strive to supplement our lacks. It is the perfectionist with an over-developed sense of duty who suffers most acutely in this respect. The greater our sense of spiritual responsibility, the more acute the strain. Consciousness of inadequate mental equipment or insufficient training to meet the demands of our work, a feeling that our spiritual capital is too meager for the heavy drafts being made upon it, combine to bring us to breaking point.

An attitude of anxiety, the habit of worrying over things beyond our power to control, can paralyze the nerve of spiritual endeavor and set up dangerous inner tensions. With some this is a hereditary tendency which has therefore come to be accepted as inevitable. The victim knows that it is futile and incapacitating but seems powerless to break a habit which through long indulgence has become part of the life pattern. Examinations, health, affairs of the heart, language study, preparation of sermons and messages, difficult meetings or interviews, relationships with colleagues in work, each constitute one more source of anxious care. The word used by our Lord for anxious care signifies a dividing and distracting of the mind so that it is kept in a state of agitation, unable to give undivided attention to any one thing.

A condition of fear is a common cause of strain. Some people of nervous temperament are afraid of everything. Fear of new responsibilities, or of undertaking untried tasks, fills the timid soul with an agony of apprehension. Physical fear which in many cases has factual justification can have far-reaching effects on both nervous system and spiritual life. It can banish sleep and fill even waking hours with a nameless dread. Fear of failure tends to produce the very condition it seeks to avoid, for God responds to faith, not to fear. Fear and faith are mutually exclusive and cannot coexist in the same heart. The fear of man, fear of what men will think or say, brings with it not only a snare but a strain.

A wrong attitude to others is fruitful in producing tension. When an inner resentment is harbored, sometimes almost unconsciously, it can work havoc with the nervous system as will envy, jealousy, ill will, and hatred. Not without profound reason did Paul exhort that these destructive emotions be resolutely "put off," for they are sinful, soul-destroying, and health-wrecking.

When there is added to one or all of these the inevitable pressures which descend on us from so many directions, the inner stress often reaches breaking point. On the mission field, lack of time for study, correspondence, interviews, home duties, interruptions—all add their quota. The continual pressure of crowds of people in home or clinic, whether they be concerned or merely curious, deprives of necessary privacy and quiet. Add to these what Paul called "the care of all the churches," the legitimate care for souls and the spiritual welfare of "your flock of God," and you have pressures before which the mind reels and the body quails. Who can live in conditions such as these, especially in an enervating and energy-sapping tropical climate, without a sense of strain?

INEVITABLE RESULTS

It requires no physician to tell that strains and tensions of this sort will exact their toll from both body and spirit. And one uncomfortable quality of strain is that it is self-communicating. When we live under tension, others know and feel it and we are unable to impart spiritual lift to the atmosphere.

It manifests itself in *physical disabilities*. May the nervous dyspepsia, to which some are subject, have its source less in the food they eat than in the thoughts they think? The man in the street knows that ulcers and mental stress are closely related. Is not the tendency of our age to migraine and sleeplessness with consequent dependence on the appropriate tablets merely the outraged nervous system taking its revenge on us for submitting it to strains God never intended it to carry? Are not many of our supposedly nervous disorders in reality spiritual in origin? Energy which could be directed to constructive ends is wastefully dissipated.

Mental turmoil. The hymn writer prays, "I would not have the restless mind that hurries to and fro," but unresolved inner tensions inevitably produce mental unrest and turmoil. The mind is unable to give undivided attention to the things of the spirit because it is in a constant whirl. During prayer time thoughts become especially uncontrollable, swinging remorselessly to the latest source of concern as the needle to the pole. Even in sleep restlessness of body evidences the deeper restlessness of the mind.

Spiritual depression is the logical climax. How could one but be depressed when body and mind form an alliance against the spirit? This condition provides our experienced and ruthless adversary with the unique opportunity of exploiting his advantage with either fiery dart or oppressive cloud as he sees most likely to achieve his purpose. Thus the sensitive and hard-pressed soul is brought into a state of spiritual bondage—haunted with a sense of defeat, oppressed with the comparative lack of fruit in life and service.

THE PANACEA

Is there a way out of this prison house, a real possibility of deliverance? Is it merely pursuing a mirage to expect God to

> Take from our lives the strain and stress
> And let our ordered lives confess
> The beauty of His peace?

There is a "way to escape" which will be found by those who are prepared to be ruthlessly honest with themselves and God, and who are deeply in earnest in their search for the key. It would seem that the following steps will need to be taken along the road to deliverance.

A rediscovery of God. Nothing less than this will meet the deepest need of our complex personality. God Himself is the answer and He will grant us this revelation of Himself when we are truly ready for what it involves. To the saints of past ages He granted a progressive revelation of Himself exactly suited to their present pressing need. What we need is a fresh revelation of Him as El Shaddai, *God* ALL-SUFFICIENT, immeasurably greater than our conscious inadequacy. Our trouble is that our God is too small, or rather that our conception and knowledge of our God are too small. He is inadequate to cope with the complexities and weaknesses of our nature. We must have a larger God. Magnifying our insufficiency instead of laying hold of His abundant resources is not only harmful but sinful for "that which is not of faith is sin." Did not Moses' harping on his insufficiency provoke God to anger (Exod 4:14)? His attitude implied that the God who had called could not be trusted to provide him with the equipment necessary to fulfill his responsibilities.

We will discover a larger God through meditation on His Word, and this takes time. There is no easy short cut. Ponder such amazing assertions as Ephesians 1:3; II Peter 1:3; I Corinthians 3:21. Believe in the availability of these resources, more than sufficient for our every lack. He who knows our need has made abundant provision for it, whether it be in the realm of the body, the mind, or the soul. The disciples' lack of bread to feed the hungry multitude did not take Him by surprise. "He himself knew what he would do"—He always does. To regain such a confidence in our great God cannot but eliminate strain, for tensions develop only when we have an inadequate God.

A recognition of self as the villain of the piece, the center and source of strain, will help us further along the road to deliverance. Do we often feel that more is being asked of us either by God or man than we are able to bear? But this is just not true, for our God assures us that He "will not suffer you to be tempted [tested] above that ye are able" (I Cor. 10:13). He knows our load limit. If, as the Scriptures teach and we profess to believe, there are no second causes, then we shall be able for all of God's commands. "If . . . God command thee so, then thou shalt be able" (Exod. 18:23) is an abiding principle. Do we complain that there are not sufficient hours in the day for all we have to do? Yet Jesus said: "Are there not twelve hours in the day?" This clearly implies that for every task we have to fulfill there is the time to fulfill it. It is more than probable that some of our numerous activities are self-imposed rather than divinely ordered, and should therefore be discontinued.

When we loudly depreciate ourselves and our capacities, does not our insincerity become apparent when we hear someone else say the very same things about us? Are we not often more anxious to secure the approbation of men than the praise of God? And does not a great deal of the strain lie in our endeavor to keep up spiritual appearances so that we may obtain it? Are we not prone to indulge self-pity and are frequently and vocally sorry for ourselves and our hard lot? Yet in His startling words to Peter, Jesus made it clear that self-pity was satanic in origin (Matt. 16:23).

Self is indeed the villain in the piece, and the real root of our trouble is that self has not abdicated the throne of our hearts in favor of Christ. When His flag flies over the citadel of Mansoul, strain gives place to serenity.

A renewal of mind is a third step toward deliverance. There must be a radical change of attitude, a genuine renewal of mind if there is to be lasting deliverance. So long as the mental attitude remains unchanged, the tension will continue. Instead of pitying and excusing ourselves because of the pressures under which we labor, we must view them no longer as amiable and unavoidable infirmities but as culpable and unnecessary sins. We will view them no longer as a burden which will crush us but as a platform for the display of His glorious sufficiency. We will hear Him say: "Now shalt thou see what I will do" (Exod. 6:1), now that our eyes are off ourselves and fixed on God. The greater our weakness, the greater glory will be His as we work in His power.

But how does this change of attitude, this renewal of mind, come? How can we induce it? It is the outcome of *a definite, purposeful choice of the will.* Do you *choose* to transfer all the burden of responsibility to Christ and to leave it there? Do you *choose* to have done forever with anxiety and fear? Then Paul exhorts: "Be renewed in the spirit of your mind" (Eph. 4:23), and "be ye transformed by the renewing of your mind" (Rom. 12:2). This is obviously not something we can do, but something God will do within us in response to our faith, and Titus 3:5 indicates that it is the work of the Holy Spirit. When we are willing once and for all to cease excusing and exonerating

ourselves and to cast ourselves wholly upon God,
then the way is open for the Holy Spirit to work
the miracle of renewing our minds. We will so
look on things as to magnify our glorious Lord and
His boundless resources, and even to rejoice in our
infirmities when they afford Him the opportunity
of displaying "His more than sufficient grace." In
other words, the Holy Spirit will work in us "the
mind which was in Christ Jesus" in ever-increasing
measure. That this would be supernatural is true,
but is not Christianity a supernatural religion from
beginning to end? We may expect the Holy Spirit
to make real to us *the reinforcing presence of the
Lord Jesus,* who dwells within to meet the daily
and hourly needs of the soul and remove every
tension and strain. Did He not promise: "Come
unto me . . . and I will give you rest"—heart rest?

Regular relaxation and quietness will make a
valuable contribution on the physical plane. "Be
still, and know that I am God" (Ps. 46:10) is a
prescription we heed too little in these days of rush.
"One of the ways in which man brings the most
trouble upon himself is by his inability to be still,"
wrote Pascal. We are busier than God intends us
to be if we are too busy to take time for relaxation.
The Lord Jesus constantly sought the stillness of
the mountaintop. He impressed upon His disciples
the necessity of coming apart for relaxation and we
disregard His counsel to our own loss. Let us covet
the ability to move from one duty to another
with a leisured heart.

One of God's gentlemen recently concluded his
prayer with a self-revealing sentence: "And so we

go blithely into the new day." Blithely! No sense of strain, no quivering tension—only a heart at perfect rest in a God who is sufficient.

2

TRANSFORMATION OF THE MIND

Let this mind be in you, which was also in Christ Jesus.—Philippians 2:5

THE MIND OF MAN is the battleground on which every moral and spiritual battle is fought. Because of its inherited bias toward sin, the natural mind is hostile to God and does not submit to God's law—"indeed, it cannot" (Rom. 8:7).

Recognizing this fatal disability, Paul counsels the believers in Rome: "Be not conformed to this world: but be ye transformed by the renewing of your mind" (Rom. 12:2). He made it his objective to bring "into captivity every thought to the obedience of Christ" (II Cor. 10:5). His challenge to the Philippians was: "Let this mind be in you, which was also in Christ Jesus" (Phil. 2:5). It should therefore be our supreme objective to have our minds so completely transformed that they will be an accurate reflection of the mind of Christ.

In the verse at the head of this chapter, Paul throws out a tremendous challenge, which he reinforces with what is probably the greatest Christological chapter in the New Testament. Different expositors have variously rendered this verse, and each translation reveals a different facet of the truth:

"Reflect in your own mind the mind of Christ." —*Lightfoot*

"Let the governing impulse of your life be the same as was in Christ Jesus." —*Cash*

"Cherish the disposition which was in Christ Jesus."

So then, the mind of Christ was His entire inner disposition, His thoughts, desires, motives, the governing impulse of His life.

Is not this the reason we Christians make so slight an impression on a cynical and materialistic world—we manifest so little of the mind, the disposition of Christ? Men see little in our lives which would make it worth while sacrificing what they already have. Dr. J. Stuart Holden expressed it: "The world does not believe in Him whom it has not seen because it has cause not to believe in us whom it has seen." Only the manifesting of the other-worldly Christ-mind in its utter contrast to the natural and carnal mind will convince men that we have something worthy of the sacrifice of all else.

This remarkable passage reveals that the Christ-mind expressed itself similarly in both His incarnate and His preincarnate state.

HIS PREINCARNATE STATE

"Who, *being in the form of God,* though it not robbery to be equal with God: but made himself of no reputation [emptied himself], and took upon him the form of a servant" (Phil. 2:6, 7). The word "form" used here refers to essential attributes, not mere external appearance; not to superficial likeness but to essential Godhead. How did the Christ-mind express itself in His pre-existent state? He did not count equality with God, with all its attendant majesty, a thing to be greedily grasped and held at all costs. Instead, He emptied Himself. By a sublime act of self-abnegation He resigned all His glories, voluntarily accepted certain limitations and veiled His majesty, that He might become Mediator between God and man. But there is no suggestion that this self-emptying involved the laying aside of His deity. The emptying is specifically said to consist in His taking the form of a slave. Being conscious of an equal place in the Godhead with the Father, He could never be other than God. But there were some things He could and did renounce. While not empty of Divine powers, He determined not to use them. Bengel's suggestion is: "He remained full, yet bore Himself as though He were empty." He voluntarily renounced the outward display of His majesty and the independent exercise of some of His attributes. Instead of a sovereign, He became a slave.

That glorious form, that light insufferable
  And that far-beaming blaze of majesty,
Wherewith He wont at Heaven's high council table
  To sit the midst of Trinal unity,
  He laid aside; and here with us to be,
Forsook the courts of everlasting day
And chose with us a darksome house of clay.

—MILTON

HIS INCARNATE STATE

He "was made in the likeness of men: and being found in fashion as a man, he humbled himself, and became obedient unto death, even the death of the cross" (Phil. 2:7, 8). He became really like men. In everything which strikes the senses—hearing, figure, actions, manner of life—He was truly man. All the weaknesses and sinless infirmities of human nature were there. And how was the Christ-mind expressed in the days of His flesh? "He humbled himself, and became obedient unto . . . the death of the cross." His inner disposition was one of utter self-abnegation and self-abandonment, even though it involved Him in the lowest depths of infamy. His humiliation involved not only giving up His place in deity, but even surrendering His place in humanity.

It is striking that each downward step which our Lord took in His humiliation would have permitted some amelioration which would have affected the validity of His atoning work. He need not have been born in a manger, lived in a laborer's home in a despised town, attended a village school, earned His living by the sweat of His face. He deliberately chose the lowliest place that He might evidence the attitude of mind He expected in His disciples.

We are to cherish and reflect the mind which brought the Son of God down from a throne of glory to a cross of shame.

This display of the mind of Christ is progressive. It began with "counting," it led to self-abasement, and it culminated in self-oblation.

These three attitudes of mind are evident in the lives of both Moses and Paul.

"Counting." Christ did not count equality with God a thing to be grasped.

Moses esteemed "the reproach of Christ greater riches than the treasures in Egypt" (Heb. 11:26).

Paul counted "all things but loss, for the excellency of the knowledge of Christ Jesus" his Lord (Phil. 3:8). The very things in which he previously took greatest pride, he counted loss for Christ (Phil. 3:7).

Everything which followed in the lives both of Paul and Moses sprang from this attitude of mind. They did not cling avidly to their rights, but gladly renounced them in the interests of others.

Self-abasement. Christ humbled Himself to take "the form of a slave."

Moses humbled himself, choosing to suffer affliction with the people of God—a horde of slaves —rather than to "enjoy the pleasures of sin for a season" (Heb. 11:25).

Paul delighted to call himself "the bondslave of Jesus Christ."

Self-oblation. Christ chose "death, even death of the cross" that a lost humanity might be redeemed.

Moses in his self-forgetful love prayed: "Oh, this people have sinned a great sin. . . . Yet now, if thou wilt forgive their sin—; and if not, blot me, I pray thee, out of thy book which thou hast written" (Exod. 32:31, 32).

Paul, in the desperation of love, wrote: "I have great heaviness and continual sorrow in my heart. For I could wish that myself were accursed from

Christ for my brethren, my kinsmen according to
the flesh" (Rom. 9:2, 3).

In these Scriptures there is a practical demonstra-
tion of the mind of Christ in men of like passions
with ourselves.

In order that we may more clearly grasp the attitude of mind which was in Christ Jesus and discover the governing impulse of His life, consider
His attitude toward things which are dearly cherished by most men and women.

The earthly mind covets and clutches at *position
and power,* and will go to all lengths to attain
them. Even in religious circles there is often an
unseemly jockeying for position which is entirely
alien to the mind of Christ, who stripped Himself
of all privilege, renounced all pomp and power,
and allowed His creatures to sneer, "Is not this the
carpenter's son?" Do we have the mind of Christ
in this?

To the earthly mind, wealth is the *summum
bonum* to be gained at any cost, even if someone
else goes to the wall in the process. Witness the
way in which the lucrative professions and busi-
nesses are rushed, even by professing Christians,
while important work for Christ, which offers
little financial return, languishes for lack of workers. When one influential and worthy pulpit in
America fell vacant, there were 250 applicants!
How unlike the mind of Christ who "though he
was rich, yet for your [our] sakes he became poor"
(II Cor. 8:9).

It is the characteristic of the earthly mind that
it always covets the *service* of others: it desires to
avoid toil and drudgery. This is one of the factors

which makes wealth so desirable—it can secure the service of others. The mind of Christ manifested itself in His words: "I am among you as he that serveth." "I came not to be ministered unto, but to minister." It was His delight to be servant of all.

Dr. Samuel Logan Brengle was a brilliant American university student, the leading orator of his year. Upon graduation he was called to the pulpit of an influential church where he was acclaimed as a coming pulpiteer. But his heart was not satisfied. He did not feel that he was reaching the people and longed to do more to spread the Gospel. At this crucial time he read of the Salvation Army, then regarded as a rather disreputable organization. But as he read of its achievements among the underprivileged people of Britain and the trophies it was winning from the gutter, he felt that this was the type of work which would satisfy his heart's yearning. He resigned his church, sailed for London, and offered his services to General William Booth. He was ultimately accepted for service, but in order to test his caliber, he was put in the training garrison with scores of cadets, most of whom, though full of zeal, were innocent of formal education.

His first work was to clean a pile of muddy boots belonging to his fellow students. As he brushed away the mud, a battle royal raged in his heart. Was it for *this* that he had renounced his fashionable church and come to London? The Devil pressed the advantages he had gained, and Brengle had almost succumbed to the tempter's voice when a pregnant verse of Scripture was injected into his mind by the Holy Spirit: "He took a towel, and girded himself." In a moment he detected the subtlety of his adversary and from his heart cried, "Lord, if Thou couldest take a towel and wash the disciples' dirty feet, surely I can take a brush and clean the cadets' dirty boots." Humility triumphed, and the victory thus gained laid a foundation for a life which multiplied itself a thousandfold in a world-wide ministry. Do we evidence the mind of Christ in this respect?

The earthly mind shrinks from *suffering* or anything that would involve loss of face. But Christ actually courted these when blessing would accrue to others. He welcomed the death of a criminal on an agonizing cross, the quintessence of suffering and shame. "I have a baptism to be baptized with," He said, "and how am I straitened until it be accomplished!" (Luke 12:59). "The cup which my Father hath given me, shall I not drink it?" (John 18:11).

The Christ-mind is so essentially opposed to the earthly mind that nothing less than a complete transformation is involved in its manifestation. Where did that mind lead Him? To the cross. If we have it, where will it lead us? Just as inevitably to the cross, for nothing but the cross of Christ is sufficiently potent to work this radical transformation.

Much of the Christianity of today is cross-less. The offense of the cross has ceased. No longer does it cut deeply into our way of life. Like the Greeks of our Lord's day, the watchwords of our philosophy are self-culture and self-enjoyment. The mind of Christ involves self-oblation and self-sacrifice, notes which are too often absent from the harmony of our lives. When Jesus became "obedient unto the death of the cross," it seemed as though this was the untimely termination of His life. Instead, it was really its germination. The single grain of wheat which fell into the ground and died on Calvary, germinated—lived again—in three thousand lives on the Day of Pentecost and in untold millions in subsequent ages.

There is no other law of spiritual fruitfulness. We must be prepared to die once and for all to do the things which appear indispensable to the earthly mind. Only as we consent to die will we live again in others. To take up the cross daily and follow our Master in self-abasement and self-oblation may not seem an alluring prospect, but when we dare to do it we will find, with Samuel Rutherford, that the cross will be to us just such a burden as wings to a bird.

How are we to obtain the mind of Christ? Can we generate it from within? Is it a process of imitation? Who could imitate the grand, majestic, crystal-pure character of Christ? Who could imitate a Raphael? Is not the secret hinted at in the exhortation, "Let this mind be in you, which was also in Christ Jesus"? It is the work of Another. Is not the supreme work of the Holy Spirit to reproduce in the yielded believer the inner disposition of Christ? What is the fruit of the Spirit (Gal. 5:22, 23) but the mind of Christ? As we willingly consent to the crucifixion of the earthly mind and purposefully yield to the sanctifying influences of the Holy Spirit, He will perform the miracle. Our minds will be transformed in ever-increasing degree by the renewing of the Holy Spirit.

3

THE PURPOSE OF SUFFERING

The third heaven . . . a thorn.
—II Corinthians 12:2, 7

It is a peculiar and precious feature of the New Testament revelation . . . that it comes to us so largely through the sacred channel of the human heart, the human personality. It does not descend in oracular thunder from the clouds. It is conveyed in large measure through a series of letters, signed with men's names, and speaking in the dialect of man's soul, and now particularly in the dialect of this man's soul, so deeply capacious of grief, of hope, of weariness, of eagerness, of longing, and of love.
—BISHOP H. G. MOULE, on II Timothy

IN THE PARAGRAPH before us (II Cor. 12:1-10) we are granted an intimate glimpse into the sanctuary of Paul's inner life. For this privilege we have to thank the cavilers whose repeated challenge to his apostleship compelled Paul to bare his heart (v. 11). Robert Louis Stevenson, although a very sick man wrote, "I should think myself a trifler and in bad taste if I introduced the world to these unimportant privacies." Paul surely exercised the same manly constraint, and it was only the necessity of vindicating his office which induced him to share such intimacies with his beloved Corinthians, and through them with us. The deepest experiences are those most rarely revealed by a man of deep sensitivity. In his defense Paul tells of two conflicting experiences, one with temptation to exaltation, and the other with its tendency to depression. Then he shows how these contrasting experiences were brought into equilibrium by a single sentence from the Lord of glory.

"THE THIRD HEAVEN"

If we follow the clue in verse 2, it would appear that Paul's third-heaven experience occurred about the time of his first missionary expedition. It could have been when he was left for dead at Lystra.

There are some rare and radiant experiences which cannot be compassed in human language, and this was one of them. Paul was transported into the realm where God is in full manifestation, and "he there heard utterances unutterable, beyond the power of man to shape into words" (v. 4). But such an ecstatic experience carried its own dangers for God's chosen messenger, dangers with which He had His own method of dealing. That Paul was in extreme peril of succumbing to spiritual pride is clear from his own statement, "Lest I should be exalted above measure" (v. 7). Nothing so tends to inflate a man with a sense of his own importance as the possession of great gifts of intellect and the enjoyment of special and unusual experiences. And there is nothing which more surely disqualifies from spiritual usefulness than spiritual pride. The very abundance of the revelations granted to Paul could easily have isolated him from the very people to whom he was sent to minister, so God brought an equalizing factor into his life lest his ministry be limited.

There is a very real danger in recounting to others our own deeper spiritual experiences, and especially our spiritual successes. There are times when it is right to do so, but it should always be with a careful scrutiny of motives. Aware of this, an evangelist greatly used of God for fifty years declined the request to tell the remarkable story of his life. He realized the subtle temptation to filch some of the glory which belonged to God alone. So jealous was he that the power of the Spirit might continue to rest on him that he made the practice of trying to forget previous victories.

It will be recalled that the favored three disciples were not permitted to encamp on the Mount of Transfiguration. They must exchange the vision glorious for the convulsions of a demon-possessed boy. So must Paul descend into the valley if he is to be God's messenger to a distraught humanity. He must learn that the mountain is only as high as the valley is deep. The higher he ascends in spiritual experience, the more deeply must he be identified with his crucified Lord.

"A THORN"

There is a studied reticence in this autobiographical glimpse. With set purpose the apostle is silent as to the location or character of the third heaven, of the words he heard, and of the vision he saw. He was equally uncommunicative concerning the nature of his thorn. We should be grateful that he thus turns our thoughts away from the incidental and concentrates our whole attention on unchanging principles of universal application. Had he specified his own personal thorn which differed from ours, we would be less ready to believe that the Divine compensation he enjoyed might be ours also. In the plan of God, his was to be a representative case from which believers of all time could draw comfort and strength.

The word *thorn* means a "splinter, stake, thorn," and has been thought to convey the painful idea of a stake on which he was impaled. As to its nature, there have been many equally inconclusive guesses—ophthalmia, malaria, migraine, epilepsy, an impediment in his speech, his unimpressive bodily presence—but suffice it to say it was something acutely painful, something either physical or temperamental, for God would never have refused to answer a prayer for the removal of something morally or spiritually evil. Whatever it was, it hurt, humiliated, and restricted him. At first he viewed it as a limiting handicap, but later, when he saw it in its true perspective, he came to regard it as a heavenly advantage.

Feeling it to be a hindrance to the fulfillment of his ministry, Paul began to pray impulsively and persistently for its removal. "I besought the Lord thrice," he confessed. He did not stop to inquire of God why it was there—he only wanted it to depart for good and all. His was no desultory request but a deep heart cry, for his thorn was causing him acute suffering, buffeting him. He acted as though it was purposeless pain, sent out of caprice. He had not yet learned that there is no such thing as purposeless pain to God's children and that He never acts out of caprice.

But now Paul found himself face to face with the problem of unanswered prayer. Was God unsympathetic to his plea? Although He did not answer the specific words of his request, He did respond to the cry of his heart. Paul's deepest desire was that his ministry should not be hindered by this thorn. God answered by assuring him that his ministry would be enriched if the thorn remained.

Monica, mother of St. Augustine, prayed importunately that her profligate son might not go to Rome, then a moral cesspool, lest he drift yet further into sin. But her specific request was unanswered. Yet Augustine's journey proved to be the first step to Milan, where he was apprehended by the Lord. This is sometimes God's method. "We ask for strength that we might achieve; we are made weak that we might obey. We ask for health that we may do greater things; we are given infirmity that we may do things better. We ask for power that we may win the praise of men; we are given weakness that we may feel our need of God. We ask for all things that we may enjoy life; we are given life that we may enjoy all things."

A DIVINE GIFT

From his own costly experience Paul affirmed that his thorn was a Divine gift. "There was *given* to me a thorn," he says, and the thought behind the word is "given as a favor"! True, Satan had a part in his testing, for he describes it as a messenger of Satan sent to buffet me (v. 7). It was not God who instigated the test, but apparently, as in the case of Job, He permitted Satan to sift His servant, and by the time the testing thorn reached Paul, it had become not "a messenger of Satan" but a gift of God's grace. It was given to him, not imposed upon him. What appeared to be the expression of the malice of Satan proved to be the beneficent gift of God, with a view to Paul's wider ministry. God's love is long-sighted. To Him the spiritual welfare and growth of His children is of far greater importance than their physical comfort; hence the ministry of suffering. He does not always spare present pain if it will produce eternal profit. "All chastening seemeth for the present to be not joyous; yet afterward it yieldeth the peaceable fruit unto them that have been exercised thereby, even the fruit of righteousness" (Heb. 12:11, A.S.V.).

Our personal thorn may be a physical limitation, a bodily deformity, a temperamental weakness, a mental handicap. To the great Dr. Alexander Whyte, the fact that he was an illegitimate child was a lifelong thorn, but how greatly it developed his sympathy and enriched his ministry! The main point for us is whether or not we have recognized in our particular thorn a gift of God's favor, or like Paul are endeavoring to thrust it from us.

It is to be noted that Paul did not manufacture his own thorn. The thorn is not always God's method of disciplining His children. We are not called to become spiritual fakirs, making beds of spikes for ourselves as some are inclined to do. It will be time enough for us to embrace the thorn when God gives it to us.

A DIVINE PURPOSE

Paul discerned in his continuing trial a Divine purpose: "lest I should be exalted above measure" (v. 7). Few of us can carry a full cup. Knowing the special temptations to pride which would beset His greatly gifted messenger, God purposed to save him from spiritual shipwreck. Once Paul perceived that the thorn he had been importuning God to remove was part of the Divine purpose of his life, his whole attitude changed. Never again does the petition fall from his lips. And what transformed the importunate suppliant into the submissive sufferer? A word from God. *"He* said unto me . . ." Paul afforded God the opportunity to speak to him, and when the voice of God distilled on his soul in the quietness of the secret place, the tumult died. Now he was ready to embrace the will of God with a song, not a sigh. Have we perceived the gracious Divine purpose in our thorn?

A DIVINE COMPENSATION

The voice of God conveyed to Paul the assurance of a Divine compensation: "My grace is sufficient for thee: for my power is made perfect in weakness" (v. 9, A.S.V.). Although the thorn was not to be removed, an equalizing and compensating factor was the gift of adequate grace and power. We never know what is in us until we are placed in the furnace of affliction, nor do we fully know and draw upon the provision of His grace. Gold is refined only in the fire, but God's fire never hurts His saints—it makes them. Blessed fire which secures the companionship of the Son of God! "My grace"—My love in action—"is sufficient for you." It was not a promise of grace for which Paul was to plead, but a bestowal of grace upon which he was to draw.

When Prebendary Webb-Peploe, one of the greatest Bible teachers of the early English Keswick Convention, was a young man, one of his dearly loved children died suddenly while the family was at the seaside. Returning from the funeral, the stricken father knelt in his study, pleading with God to make His grace sufficient in this hour of sorrow. But no comfort came to his heart and the tears continued to flow. Even the Word of God had no message for him. After some time, through his tears he read again the text which had for long hung over his mantelpiece. For the first time he noticed one word printed in large capitals. "My grace IS sufficient for thee," he read with anointed eyes. "Lord, forgive me," he cried. "I have been asking Thee to make Thy grace sufficient for me, and all the time Thou hast been saying to me, 'My grace *is* sufficient for thee.' I thank Thee for sufficient grace and I appropriate it now."

God's grace is not only adequate but it is also available for every time of need. We do not need to ask for it. It has already been given and it only remains for us to receive it. What a spacious statement this is, how wide its scope! Grace sufficient in a mistaken marriage, in uncongenial employment, in an unsympathetic home, in physical weakness and pain, in the pressures of missionary life, in crushing grief. Our disabilities are blessings in disguise if they cause us to lay hold on God's sufficient grace.

Paul affords us a magnificent example in his reactions to the Divine disciplines. "Most *gladly* therefore will I rather glory in my infirmities" (v. 9), he confidently affirms. The thorn had lost none of its sharpness nor had the buffeting become any less severe, but the compensating grace of God had enabled him to turn the doleful dirge into a song of triumph.

The world's philosophy is "What can't be cured must be endured." But Paul radiantly testifies, "What can't be cured can be enjoyed. I even enjoy weakness, sufferings, privations, and difficulties." So wonderful did he prove God's grace to be that he even welcomed fresh occasions of drawing upon its fullness. "I gladly glory . . . I even enjoy"—my thorn.

Her biographer paid a remarkable tribute to the triumphant faith of Emma Piechynska, wife of a Polish nobleman, whose life was one long frustration and disappointment. It was this: "She made magnificent bouquets out of the refusals of God."

Finally, Paul discovered that through the experiences of the thorn, he was not only delivered from the peril of spiritual pride, but new reservoirs of spiritual power became available to him. He was able to exchange his weakness for Divine power. God's power did not dispel his weakness; rather it was perfected in it. "My strength is made perfect in [your] weakness," was God's statement.

Instead of pleading his suffering and pain as an

excuse from sacrificial service, or even asking for its removal, Paul now laid hold on the adequate grace and power of God and attempted greater exploits for Him than ever before. He turned the weapon with which Satan had tried to lay him low against his adversary and gained a glorious victory for his Lord. Thus the rapturous experience of the third heaven paled before the glorious compensation of the troublesome thorn.

4

DESPONDENCY, ITS CAUSE
AND CURE

Take away my life.

Kill me, I pray thee, out of hand.—Numbers
11:15
O Lord, take away my life.—I Kings 19:4
O Lord, take ... my life from me.—Jonah 4:3

IT IS COMMON KNOWLEDGE that there are today
more cases of nervous breakdown and mental
depression than ever before in history—doubtless
a legacy of two world wars and the continuous state
of tension in which we now live. The servants of
God are not promised immunity from periods of
despondency if they violate natural and spiritual
laws, nor have they ever been, as a study of the
Scriptures will reveal.

The Christian has a very astute adversary whose
threefold objective, in the apt words of Miss Ruth
Paxson, is to despoil him of his wealth, decoy him
from his walk, and disable him for his warfare.
What better weapon can he use for this purpose
than despondency and depression? Who among
us has not experienced that nameless feeling of
misery and hopelessness—indefinable, yet so des-

perately real? There is comfort for us in the realization that we are not alone in this experience, that men and women of God have trodden the same shadowed pathway before us, and that there is a way of deliverance for us as there was for them.

THE DEEPS OF DESPONDENCY

Is it not significant that each of the men in the Scripture record who prayed for death was an outstandingly successful prophet? Perhaps their very prominence was God's reason for selecting them as examples to us lesser mortals. It is a serious case of depression indeed which robs a believer of his desire to live, and it must have deep-seated causes.

MOSES the meek had achieved stupendous things for God and his nation, and for long had carried unbelievable burdens. Under his leadership a rabble of slaves had become an organized nation. They had experienced God's miraculous care and provision time and again, but their perpetual discontent and rebellion against Him so oppressed Moses that he cried out in anguish: "I am not able to bear all this people alone . . . kill me . . . let me not see my wretchedness." Overburdened with the fickleness of man, he had reached and passed the limit of endurance and was overwhelmed with a sense of complete and utter failure. He overlooked the fact that God has made us responsible for our own perfection, not for that of others. He little dreamed that many years of wonderful service lay ahead of him.

ELIJAH was fresh from the most dramatic scene of a generation in which he had figured as the Divine instrument in the destruction of the prophets of Baal. Then suddenly he wilted, his amazing courage failed, and he fled from the face of the woman he so recently had defied. Under the lonely juniper tree he mourned: "O Lord, take away my life; for I am not better than my fathers."

After his craven flight and submarine experience, JONAH had repented and returned, delivered God's message to wicked Nineveh, and to his amazement and dismay had seen that vast city turn to God, repenting in dust and ashes. But instead of leaping for joy he drooped under the gourd and moaned: "O Lord, take, I beseech thee my life from me; for it is better for me to die than to live."

THE INCIDENCE OF DESPONDENCY

Consideration of the circumstances surrounding the unanswered prayers of these men reveals the surprising fact that in each case they had more reason for elation than depression. Had Moses not seen God's mighty power working through His instrumentality, both in Egypt and in the wilderness? Had Elijah not witnessed the visible manifestation of the presence of God on Carmel, with the resulting prostration and confession of the apostate nation? Had Jonah not been the instrument of the greatest mass-turning to God recorded in human history? Then why despondency and despair?

The fact is that we never know when the adversary will launch this devastating guided missile against us. It may come when there seems least reason for it, but generally there are conditions precedent which account for its advent.

THE DIAGNOSIS OF DESPONDENCY

It would appear that in the case of each of the men we are considering, there was a threefold background to their despondency.

Physiological. The physical endurance of Moses was overtaxed by the unremitting strain of his daily administration and adjudication. Virtue—heart energy—was constantly going out of him as he heard the people's disputes and advised on their problems. To maintain liaison between God and a nation of two million discontented people was a superhuman task. With keen discernment, his father-in-law Jethro saw that Moses was being worn away in his noble attempts to fulfill his ministry. We ourselves are not always the best judges of the cost at which we do our work, and often fail to realize that our physical and nervous resources are seriously drained. Although we may not always appreciate the advice of our Jethros, they may be God's messengers to us, to whom we do well to pay heed.

Then consider the emotional stress and strain of Elijah's lone encounter on Carmel, the intensity of his praying, the thirty-mile run to Jezreel, the subsequent flight from Jezebel, and his abstinence from food. He was exhausted, emotionally and physically, and totally unfit to meet the threats of the raging Jezebel.

Jonah's depression too had a physical basis. C. C. Dobson sees in God's method of dealing with Jonah a clue to its cause—a touch of sunstroke. Emotionally spent and physically exhausted after his witness to a city as large as Philadelphia or

Sydney, and apparently affected by the heat of the sun, Jonah limped out of the city and erected a shelter from the sun's burning rays. But after the divinely prepared gourd had withered, "the sun beat upon the head of Jonah, that he fainted" (4:8).

Such were the physical causes, but with each prophet there was yet another reason for despondency.

Selfish. Until the very moment of his collapse, Moses had been singularly selfless in his care of his people. Indeed, when the anger of God was kindled against the idolatrous people, Moses had asked that his name be blotted out of God's Book, if only they might be spared. But now he dropped to a lower plane (Num. 11:11-15). Forgetting the desperate spiritual need of the people, he reproached God and indulged in an orgy of self-pity. He lost sight of all that God had enabled him to achieve and became self-engrossed.

Elijah too, in his time of reaction, reproached God and in strange self-disillusionment cried: "I am not better than my fathers." His self-esteem had been dealt a shattering blow. "I have been very jealous for the Lord God," he complained, implying that in spite of his zeal, he had been "let down." His twice repeated, "I, even I only, am left," indicates his sense of loneliness in his devotion to God. He too was engulfed in self-pity.

Nor was the case different with Jonah. His cause for reproaching God was a resentment of His grace and forbearance! The real trouble was that God's goodness to Nineveh had shattered his reputation as a prophet. Jonah had prophesied judgment, and God had exercised mercy. Since his reputation was gone, Jonah concluded that it would be better to die than to live.

In each case the desire to die stemmed from making self and self-interest supreme instead of God and His glory. Is not all despondency in essence a manifestation of self in one form or another?

Spiritual. But these were all true men of God, and neither the physical nor selfish was the sole cause of their depression. In each case there was a deep spiritual disappointment, a sense of failure. Beneath Moses' outburst lay a sense of being out of touch with God (Num 11:11), a not infrequent feeling at such a time. Coupled with this was keen disappointment at the renewed discontent and murmuring of the Israelites against God. He was a failure, too small for the task. He despaired of ever carrying out God's purpose. Better to die than to witness the failure of the whole project.

Elijah had longed and prayed for a sweeping and permanent revival of true religion in Israel, but the fair promise of Carmel had vanished once the long-denied rain had fallen. The stirring had been only superficial and evanescent, and he was still absolutely alone, he thought, in his zeal for God's cause. His courageous witness on Carmel, on which he had banked so much, had apparently been futile. He was a failure, and death was preferable to life under such conditions.

Jonah's repentance and subsequent prophetic ministry to mighty Nineveh had been a noble and costly effort. He had obeyed the Lord, delivering the warning message that in forty days Nineveh would be overthrown because of its wickedness. And then, because they had repented, God had changed His mind and let him down. How could he ever face the people again? And the worst of it was, that in his heart he had known God would do this, for he himself had experienced God's grace and forbearance. How could he be sure of his message again? He was a failure as a prophet and might just as well end it all.

THE DIVINE PRESCRIPTION

God's dealings with each of His overwrought servants is a gracious unveiling of His tender and personal discrimination. In not one case did He answer their prayers, for He perceived their true motive and realized that the petition was merely the expression of temporary self-pity. For each He had His own certain remedy.

For Moses He prescribed the help of seventy Spirit-endued elders who would share his burden and leave him free for his spiritual ministry. He quelled the murmuring of the people by granting their hearts' desire, albeit at the cost of leanness to their own souls. He renewed His reassuring promise (Num. 11:23) and gave Moses a fresh commission.

The treatment for Elijah was, first, withdrawal to a solitary place where God could speak to him alone, and reveal Himself afresh. Then two long sleeps, two meals of bread baked in God's kitchen, and long draughts of water drawn from the wells of Heaven. There followed the encouraging assurance that, far from being alone, Elijah had the moral support of seven thousand others who had never bowed the knee to Baal, and of these one was given him for a companion.

For Jonah the Lord prepared a sheltering goúrd and, through his petulant pity for the gourd when it withered, revealed to him the Divine solicitude and pity for the inhabitants of the now repentant Nineveh.

LESSONS FOR TODAY

The biographies of God's heroes are written for our instruction and encouragement, and the episodes we have been studying are replete with lessons singularly appropriate to our needs today. Even God's honored servants cannot break His physical laws with impunity, nor are they immune from the onslaughts of despondency.

Overexpenditure of physical and nervous capital, even in desperately needy areas of the Lord's service, gives the adversary opportunity to attack our spirits. We overspend at our peril.

Despondency can follow spiritual success as easily as spiritual failure.

We must seek physical and spiritual renewal if we are not to be put to flight by our enemy.

If we shift our center from God to self, even for a period, we lay ourselves open to this malady of the spirit.

We should give weight to the advice of our Jethros. Delegation of work and dropping of some commitments can bring a speedy resurgence of spiritual optimism.

Physical precautions can prevent sunstroke—or malaria, not to mention neurasthenia and heart afflictions.

Discouragement over the apparent failure of our best efforts, if not met with the shield of faith, will react disastrously on our spirits and degenerate into self-pity and despair.

Such failure is sometimes more apparent than real—as with Elijah and the seven thousand.

Going to bed early and a change of diet will settle many a case of depression. "I have so much to do," said the French philosopher Le Maistre, "that I must go to bed."

God prescribes individually for each of His patients.

God delights to restore each depressed soul to a sphere of increased usefulness.

"Above all, taking the shield of faith, wherewith ye shall be able to quench all the fiery darts of the wicked" (Eph. 6:16).

5

SPIRITUAL DECLINE AND
RECOVERY

*Gray hairs are here and there upon him, yet he
knoweth not.*—Hosea 7:9

O Israel, return unto the Lord thy God; for
thou hast fallen by thine iniquity. Take with
you words, and turn to the Lord: say unto him,
Take away all iniquity, and receive us graciously: so will we render the calves of our lips.
Asshur shall not save us; we will not ride upon
horses; neither will we say any more to the
work of our hands, Ye are our gods: for in thee
the fatherless findeth mercy. I will heal their
backsliding, I will love them freely: for mine
anger is turned away from him.—Hosea 14:1-4

IT IS EASY to get out of vital touch with God.
This loss of spiritual adjustment is not always
deliberate but it is none the less tragic in its results if the condition is not dealt with. It is this
possibility which is in view in the prayer of Hebrews 13:20, 21: "The God of peace . . . make
you perfect . . ." The idea of the latter clause is to
"put you into correct adjustment" and can be il-
lustrated by a dislocated arm. Its urgent need is

to be put back into adjustment with the rest of the body. Only then will the vital force of the body empower it for its true function. Perhaps our present need is to be put back into correct spiritual adjustment so that we can fulfill our true function in the Body of Christ.

The message of the prophet Hosea, tenderest of all the prophecies, had this end in view. It sprang from the depths of his own domestic tragedy, hence its pathos and tenderness. The passages with which we are concerned refer to Ephraim—used here of the whole kingdom of Israel of which Ephraim was the dominant tribe—and constitute a Divine diagnosis of the cause of their spiritual decline.

PERIL OF SUPERFICIAL CONSECRATION

"O Ephraim, what shall I do unto thee? . . . For your goodness is as a morning cloud, and as the early dew it goeth away" (6:4).

We live in an age characterized by superficiality, and it is consequently easy for us to be superficial in our reactions to God's message. We seldom give God time to deal with us radically and deeply. Even when we experience conviction of failure and sin, we do not allow the Holy Spirit to work in us so strongly that we are brought to hate the sin. We lightly assent to our sinfulness without seriously and permanently dealing with it. We act as though new resolves would take the place of heart repentance and renunciation. God's complaint was that Ephraim's goodness was volatile, disappearing like the morning cloud and the early dew. It is not that we do not want the best and the highest, or that we do not resolve to do better, but our resolves are evanescent.

It would seem as though Ephraim's fickleness puzzled even God, causing Him to exclaim, "O Ephraim, what shall I do unto thee?" And our fickleness and superficiality too must perplex God. But we can remember for our encouragement that Simon the Volatile, under the influence of the Holy Spirit, was transformed into Peter the Rock.

PERIL OF PARTIAL SANCTIFICATION

"Ephraim is a cake not turned" (7:8). This was a pictorial figure familiar to Israel. What housewife has not had the humiliating experience of a cake cooked on the outside but half-raw within? The cake referred to here was cooked on a griddle, and not having been turned, it was burned on one side and raw on the other. Many are like this in character—overdeveloped in some respects but deficient in others. Progress has been excellent in some areas but retarded in others. All of us to some extent are only partially sanctified, because we have not turned some parts of our lives toward the fire of the Holy Spirit. Some are strong in Bible knowledge but weak in spiritual grace. Some are generous in nature but violent in temper. Some are strong for orthodoxy but weak in Christian love. One-sided development is true of us all. Jesus alone was completely sanctified and truly symmetrical in character, "full of grace and truth." In Him we see in perfect balance "the goodness and severity of God." It could never be said of Him that He was "a cake not turned."

It is a common temptation to overdo some forms

of work which we like, but to neglect hidden and less congenial tasks. We tend to cultivate our strong points and to neglect our weak ones. The scholar avidly feeds his mind but neglects his body. Scripture enjoins the cultivation of the weak points in our characters, so that we may "stand perfect and complete in all the will of God."

The reassuring fact for us is that the fire under the cake still burns. There is yet time for the cake to be turned and for the baking process to be completed. It is for us to turn the imperfect, unfinished part of our characters toward the fire of the Spirit and allow Him to sanctify us wholly.

PERIL OF INCOMPLETE SEPARATION

"Ephraim is joined to idols: let him alone" (4:17). "Ephraim, he hath mixed himself among the people" (7:8). There is wrong separation which so puts us out of touch with worldly people that we cannot reach them for Christ. When Jesus said, "Ye are the salt of the earth," He did not have in mind the salt being on one plate and the meat on the other. He never suggested that Christians should isolate themselves and leave the world for the Devil. He Himself was the object of criticism by the Pharisees because He refused to practice this form of separation. "This man receiveth sinners, and eateth with them," they sneered.

But there is a separation which is not only right but obligatory. Ephraim must separate himself from his idols, must separate himself from the ungodly nations. The statement concerning Ephraim and his idols is frequently misread, as though God were saying, "Well, if Ephraim *will* have his idols,

let him have them! I am through with him." But
that is exactly what God is not saying. "How shall
I give thee up, Ephraim?" is the lament of God.
(11:8). It was not that God was going to leave
Ephraim alone, but He was warning Judah not to
follow this evil example of idolatry. "If he will go
after his idols, don't you follow him." It is all too
easy to slavishly follow others into the world or in
the adoption of lower standards. "Let him alone"
is the Divine warning. There are some associations
with the world which must be broken, but it is to
be the separation of insulation rather than isola-
tion. Our Lord was "separate from sinners," but
His separation was moral and spiritual, not physical.

PERIL OF UNCONSCIOUS DETERIORATION

"Strangers have devoured his strength, and he
knoweth it not; yea, gray hairs are here and there
upon him, yet he knoweth not" (7:9).

Gray hairs, sign of waning physical virility,
come unfelt and unknown. Few go gray in a night.
Spiritual decline is not necessarily conscious or sud-
den. Backsliding is not usually determined and
deliberate. Spiritual vision and enthusiasm always
tend to wane. Ephraim's deterioration began with
an unholy alliance which led to idolatry. "Asshur
[Assyria] shall not save us; we will not ride upon
horses: neither will we say any more to the work
of our hands, Ye are our gods" (14:3). As always,
idolatry led to immorality, with the consequent
weakening of the whole fabric of the nation.

The warning is plain, and we should be at pains
to discover whether signs of premature old age

are appearing in our spiritual lives. It is possible
that we are merely keeping up appearances while
spiritual atrophy is already far advanced. Ignorance
of our true state may be the result of our having
neglected to look searchingly at ourselves in the
mirror of the Word of God. The mirror would reveal to us, if we cared to see it, the tremendous
difference between the ideal and the actual. Backsliding frequently begins when we are too busy to
measure ourselves by the Divine standard.

The tradegy of Ephraim's condition was "he
knoweth not." "Samson wist not that the Lord was
departed from him"—tragic and unnecessary ignorance.

The only satisfactory and permanent way to dispose of gray hairs is not to dye them but to pull
them out by the roots. The Corinthian Christians
were commanded: *"Cleanse ourselves {yourselves}
from all filthiness of the flesh and spirit"* (II Cor.
7:1). There is a cleansing, a plucking out which
God cannot do for us. When we have done our
part, then He responds: "From all your filthiness,
and from all your idols, will I cleanse you" (Ezek.
36:25).

THE DIVINE REMEDY

God does not stop with a diagnosis of the malady, but graciously prescribes the cure, which is
the same for us as for Ephraim.

First, He enjoins *repentance*—not a vague and
general confession but a specific and personal out-
pouring of a contrite heart. "Take with you words
... say unto him, Take away all iniquity" (14:2).

Our sins have been committed individually, and it is right that we should name them before Him.

Then there is to be *renunciation* of entangling alliances. Association with the ruthless Assyrians and dependence on the forbidden Egyptian horses had been Ephraim's undoing. Such alliances must be forever done with. Say "Asshur [Assyria] shall not save us; we will not ride upon horses" (14:3). And there must be complete renunciation of all idols: "Neither will we say any more to the work of our hands, Ye are our gods" (14:3). God will tolerate nothing in the life which takes the supreme place which is His by right.

Finally, He invites Ephraim to *"turn* to the Lord" (14:2). And when he returns, what a gracious welcome awaits him from his forgiving God! "I will heal their backsliding, I will love them freely: for mine anger is turned away from him" (14:4).

RESULTING BLESSINGS

Among the blessings of restored communion and readjustment promised by God, three are prominent:

He promises *freshness.* "I will be as the dew unto Israel" (14:5). Ephraim's superficial goodness which vanished like the early dew is replaced by the refreshing dew of God. In the East, dew is the main source of renewal and without it the vegetation would die. It is not a luxury but a necessity. The readjusted life which previously had been dry and barren is now dew-drenched and fresh. All things become new by the renewing of the Holy Spirit. And the dew received will become dew imparted. "The remnant of Jacob shall be in the midst of many people as a dew from the Lord" (Micah 5:7). Our lives may be both perennially refreshed and continually refreshing others.

Then the freshness of the dew releases the *fragrance* of the flower. Freshness and fragrance belong together. When drought sets in, the scent of the flower departs. The promise through Hosea is: "They shall revive . . . the scent thereof shall be as the wine of Lebanon" (14:7). Fragrance is a subtle thing, but its absence is easily detected, and its presence cannot be mistaken. When the disciples had spent time with Jesus, they came away with His unmistakable fragrance about them and men "took knowledge of them that they had been with Jesus." His fragrance could not be hid. "But thanks be unto God, who always leadeth us in triumph in Christ, and maketh manifest through us the savor of his knowledge in every place. For we are a sweet savor of Christ unto God, in them that are saved, and in them that perish" (II Cor. 2:14, 15, A.S.V.).

But freshness and fragrance, delightful though they are, are not ends in themselves. *Fruitfulness* is the end of all nature. Hosea tells us that the same Lord who sends the dew and produces the fragrance, causes fruitfulness to spring forth. "From me is thy fruit found" (14:8). The broken branch, out of adjustment with the tree, produces no fruit to perfection. The believer who is out of adjustment with God cannot produce the fruit of the Spirit. But with correct adjustment restored, he can bring forth fruit unto God.

6

THE FUNCTION OF CONSCIENCE

I have lived in all good conscience.—Acts 23:1

IGNORANCE OF THE FUNCTION of conscience and of the Divine provision for its healthy exercise can lead to serious spiritual disorders. Many sensitive Christians have limped through life because of a morbid and weak conscience whose condemning voice allowed them no respite. Their very sincerity and desire to do the will of God only accentuated the problem and caused them to live in a state of perpetual self-accusation. Deliverance from this unhappy state is possible through the apprehension and appropriation of the teaching of Scripture on the subject. Truth is always potent to set us free.

Is conscience a separate faculty of man's moral nature? Is it a fallible human mechanism or an infallible Divine endowment? From a consideration of the relevant Scriptures it would appear to be a special activity of the intellect and feelings which enables man to judge between good and evil, to perceive moral distinctions. It has been defined as the testimony and judgment of the soul which gives approbation or disapprobation to the acts of the will. Not possessing this capacity, animals are incapable of sin. Without it, man too could not be held responsible for sin which he was incapable of discerning. It is the activity of conscience which renders man's sin culpable. The word signifies a knowledge held in conjunction with another—in this instance with God—and carries the idea of man being co-witness with God for or against himself according to his own estimate of his actions. Kant the philosopher refers to it as "the categorical imperative." Conscience is the nerve center of the soul, sensitive to moral pleasure and pain, whose function it is to adjudicate as to the moral quality of an action, and how we should act in view of it.

Conscience is not something which we gradually acquire but is part of our essential nature. It is neither supernatural nor Divine, but a purely human equipment, often described as the voice of God in the soul. But if this were true, it could never lead to sinful action. Indeed, conscience may actually be the voice of the Devil. It is not the voice of God but rather the power to hear the voice of God in the soul. Conscience originates nothing. It is like a thermometer, which though detecting and indicating the temperature, never modifies or creates its own temperature. It is the highest and most mysterious faculty in the moral nature of man and speaks with most convincing authority when habitually obeyed. "When we obey it, we live in the beatitudes. When we disobey it, like John the Baptist it cries, 'It is not lawful!' "

Paul assures us that the heathen possess conscience. They have a law within themselves which urges them to take a certain course of action or to desist from it(Rom. 2:15). An Indian in Northwest Canada picturesquely described the activity of his conscience. "It is a little three-cornered thing inside of me. When I do wrong it turns round and hurts me very much. But if I keep on doing wrong it will turn so much that the corners become worn off and it does not hurt any more."

With characteristic spiritual insight, John Bunyan in his *Holy War* represents the human family under the figure of a city, Mansoul. One of its citizens he calls Mr. Conscience. When Diabolus captured the city, he sought to destroy all trace of its former ownership by Emmanuel. Since he could not kill Mr. Conscience he sought to imprison him in a deep dungeon where his voice would be effectively silenced. But when Emmanuel undertook the recapture of Mansoul, as soon as veteran Captain Conviction led the assault upon Ear Gate, old Mr. Conscience was so aroused that he began to shout in his dungeon until the whole city was stirred at his voice, loudly recalling their allegiance to Emmanuel and condemning the rebellion against his authority.

It must be noted that conscience is not an executive faculty. It has no power to make a man do right or cease to do wrong. It delivers its judgment, produces the appropriate emotion, but leaves it to the will of man to act in the light of its verdict. It has no further power of responsibility.

LIMITATIONS OF CONSCIENCE

"I live by my conscience" is a statement sometimes made with complacency, as though that automatically rendered the resulting action right. But is conscience an infallible guide? By no means. "For I know nothing against myself," wrote Paul, "yet I am not hereby justified" (I Cor. 4:4, A.S.V.). Wordsworth erred in describing it as "God's most intimate presence in the soul and His most perfect image in the world." Paul's assertion that he had to exercise his conscience to keep it functioning correctly bears this out (Acts 24:16). It cannot therefore be infallible, but is a fluctuating factor which reacts faithfully to the standard of moral conduct to which it witnesses. That standard may be imperfect or flagrantly wrong, but such as it is, conscience will adjudicate according to it. In former times the conscience of a Hindu would protest loudly against the killing of a cow but would remain quiescent while he sacrificed his child. A Hindu once said to a British administrator: "Our conscience tells us it is right to burn our widows on the pyre of their husbands." "Yes," replied the officer, "and our conscience tells us it is right to hang you if you do." It is all a matter of the moral standard to which conscience bears witness. If the standard accepted is a wrong one, conscience will allow without protest even such abuses as the horrors of the Inquisition in the name of Christ.

The fact is that every conscience needs instruction. Its delicate mechanism has been thrown off balance by the Fall. Just as a bullet will reach the bull's-eye only if the two sights are in correct alignment, so correct moral judgments are delivered only when conscience is correctly aligned with the Scriptures. And herein lies a powerful argument for the reverent and diligent study of the whole Word of God. As a watch must be set and regulated by standard time, so conscience must be set and regulated by God's infallible standard as revealed in His Word. And of course the only norm of character is our Lord Jesus Christ. If we walk with Him our standards will be ever rising.

While conscience obediently responds to the standard of right which it knows, it is limited by custom, habit, and prejudice. These can speak so loudly that they seem to be the very voice of conscience. Custom so blunted the conscience of the southerners to the evils of slavery that only after an long and bitter education were the captives liberated. So blinded by prejudice and bigotry was Paul that he thought he was obeying the voice of God in persecuting the church. How bitterly he repented when he saw the true nature of the actions to which his conscience had assented! Often when we think we are standing for principle we are only falling for prejudice.

So then conscience when regulated by the Word of God is the monitor in the soul of man which insists on right doing, condemns wrongdoing, produces remorse when flouted, and imparts peace when heeded.

A CONDEMNING CONSCIENCE

Conscience either condemns or commends any purposed action, and Scripture lists four progressive states in each category. First let us consider the possible states of the condemning conscience which makes cowards of us all.

A *weak* conscience is one which is not healthy but morbid, overscrupulous and oversensitive (I Cor. 8:7-12). It reacts faithfully according to its light, but like a compass with a weak magnetic current it is easily influenced and tends to vacillate. Its possessor is constantly tormented by doubt as to whether an action is right or wrong and constantly digs up in unbelief what has been sown in faith. It is very possible to become a martyr to conscience, as John Wesley discovered when he one day vowed that he would not speak to a soul unless the Spirit definitely prompted him. On arriving at Kingswood at the end of the day he found he had not spoken to a soul. He then made the resolution that when there were souls needing speaking to, it would be well for him to do the speaking and trust the Holy Spirit to use the opportunity as he had followed it up.

A conscience may be weak for two reasons—an imperfect knowledge of God's Word and will, with a consequent imperfect faith, or an unsurrendered will which gives a vacillating choice. When there is obedience to the known will of God or a willingness to do that will, there is no need to be harassed by an overscrupulous conscience, and we should refuse to constantly review an action committed in good faith. Too many are given to the unsatisfying occupation of photographing themselves and developing the plates. The corrective is to clearly face the issues involved in a situation in the light of Scripture and, seeking the guidance of the Spirit, come to a decision according to one's best judgment. Thereafter resolutely refuse to reopen the matter.

A weak conscience may easily degenerate into one which is *defiled*. Its very purity makes it the more susceptible to defilement. "Some, being used now to the idol, eat as of a thing sacrificed to an idol; and their conscience being weak is defiled" (I Cor. 8:7, A.S.V.). If we persist in some action against which conscience has witnessed, we thereby defile it and thus prevent its faithful functioning. When a watch stops, it is not the fault of the watch but of the dust which has clogged its delicate mechanism. So with conscience, especially in the realm of purity. "To the pure all things are pure: but to them that are defiled and unbelieving nothing is pure; but both their mind and their conscience are defiled" (Titus 1:15, A.S.V.). Failure to heed the voice of conscience is fraught with serious consequences: "Holding . . . a good conscience; which some having thrust from them made shipwreck concerning the faith," warned Paul (I Tim. 1:19, A.S.V.).

Through constant defilement which is not cleansed away, a conscience may become habitually *evil* (Heb. 10:22). If its possessor *will* practice evil, then it will permit him to do it with less and less remonstrance. It begins to react to his lowering standards until it comes to regard evil as good and good as evil. A burglar who has been guilty of every crime on the calendar had never been troubled by his conscience over any of his crimes, but he was filled with remorse because he had spent $10.00 entrusted to him by another burglar!

Habitual defiance of the verdict of conscience cauterizes it until it is reduced to insensibility and no longer protests. When it reaches this condition, Paul describes it as *seared, cauterized,* utterly insensitive, petrified. "Speaking lies . . . their conscience seared" (I Tim. 4:2). This is a terrible condition—no appeal will succeed, for it has practically been done to death.

> Vice is a monster of such frightful mien
> That to be hated, needs but to be seen;
> But seen too oft, familiar with her face,
> We first endure, then pity, then embrace.
> —ALEXANDER POPE

Note the downward progress. A pure conscience becomes weak and defiled, but it will not remain long at this stage unless its purity is restored by renunciation of the evil and cleansing. It deteriorates further and becomes evil, permitting its possessor increasingly to practice wrong without remonstrance. The claim, "My conscience did not trouble me," is more likely to betoken an evil than a pure conscience. Then comes the final tragic state—seared.

A COMMENDING CONSCIENCE

This is a prize to be coveted above all else. "Beloved, if our heart [conscience] condemn us not, then have we confidence toward God" (I John 3:21). It is just as faithful in commending the right as in condemning the wrong. A *pure* conscience (I Tim. 3:9, II Tim. 1:3) is one which doing its duty faithfully is very sensitive to the approach of evil. A proprietor of livery stables once purchased a load of straw from a menagerie. His horses became restless and uneasy. Although they had never seen a lion, they sensed that their natural enemy had been in contact with the straw. Conscience is kept pure and sensitive as we faithfully obey the light shed on our conduct by the

Word of God. It reacts to that standard and will accept nothing short of it.

A *good* conscience is the happy possession of a person who in all things accepts the dictates of his pure conscience (I Tim. 1:5, 19). Its reproof is welcomed and acted upon by eliminating what is wrong or adding what is deficient. A pure and good conscience is one which is *"void of offense* toward God, and toward men" (Acts 24:16), a state which brings serenity and heart rest. No accusing voice shatters peace with God or mars relations with men. To forfeit this is to pay too high a price for whatever may appear to be gained. But the attaining of a conscience void of offense was for Paul a matter of constant exercise. He had a gymnasium for his soul. The height of attainment is gained when conscience is *perfected* (Heb. 9:9) through the cleansing of the blood of Christ.

A CLEANSED CONSCIENCE

But what is the panacea for a defiled and condemning conscience? Scripture indicates that twofold cleansing is necessary and possible.

"Cleanse ourselves [yourselves] from all filthiness of flesh and spirit, perfecting holiness in the fear of God" is the Divine injunction (II Cor. 7:1). Charles Darwin wrote of animals which never see because they have lost the capacity for seeing through living in a cave. He found some which had lived not too far within the cave, and while their sight was partially gone, it gradually returned as they were slowly accustomed to the light. Even though conscience may have lost much of its sensitiveness to sin, it is not too late for it to

be restored. The first step is one which we ourselves must take by cleansing—separating—ourselves from all we know to be sinful and contrary
to the will of God. If we are unwilling to do this,
we automatically disqualify ourselves from experi-
encing the cleansing of the blood of Christ. But if
we resolutely set ourselves to deal with all known
sin, we may count on the aid of the Holy Spirit to
confirm us in our purpose and enable its achievement.

But our cleansing of ourselves is only a necessary preparation for conscience being *cleansed by
the blood of Christ.* Conscience has no cure for its
own ills. Hebrews 9:13, 14 (A.S.V.) gives the
infallible prescription for its complete cleansing
and renewal. "If the blood of goats and bulls, and
the ashes of a heifer sprinkling them that have
been defiled, sanctify unto cleanness of the flesh:
how much more shall the blood of Christ . . .
cleanse your conscience from dead works?" The
characteristic of the sacrifice of the red heifer al-
luded to in this passage was that it was always
available and easily accessible. So with the cleansing of the blood of Christ. But as with the con-
science-stricken Israelite, so with us: the available
sacrifice must be personally appropriated.

> Precious, precious blood of Jesus
>   Ever flowing free;
> I believe it, I receive it,
>   'TIS FOR ME.

The forgiveness of the worst sin causes it to pass
immediately and completely from the conscience.
Never again need it haunt us. Conscience like a

released spring returns to its normal action of warning against the fresh approach of sin and adjudicating on the character of moral action. With the removal of the dead weight of past sin, the soul soars like a released lark with a song into its native element. The Holy Spirit, who applies the powerful solvent of the blood of Christ to the defiled conscience in response to our faith, delights to make it possible for us henceforth to live with a conscience "void of offense toward God, and toward men."

7

THE HOLY SPIRIT AND
OUR HANDICAPS

There is therefore now no condemnation
[disability].

There is, therefore, now no condemnation [disability] to them which are in Christ Jesus.
. . . For the law of the Spirit of life in Christ Jessu hath made me free from the law of sin and death.—Romans 8:1, 2

OUR DISABILITIES AND HANDICAPS need not limit our usefulness. We are not doomed to limp along doing our poor best, hardly to hope that the future can be better than the past. There is deliverance from all our temperamental and psychological problems. This is the optimistic and satisfying thesis of Paul the missionary in Romans 8.

Nowhere in literature, sacred or profane, is there a more poignant portrayal of the defeated life than in Romans 7. The agony of heart which approves the good but does the evil is presented in graphic pictures. "For that which I do I know not: for not what I would, that do I practice; but what I hate, that I do" (7:15, A.S.V.). "To will is present with me, but to do that which is good is not" (7:18, A.S.V.). The apostle is deeply conscious of an inversion of will. His whole will is against the involuntary sinful actions of the flesh. He does not choose them, but when the critical point in temptation arrives his will is paralyzed. The climax is reached in 7:24 (A.S.V.): "Wretched man that I am! who shall deliver me out of the body of this death?"

From the unrelieved pessimism of chapter 7 we emerge into the glorious optimism of chapter 8. "There is therefore now no condemnation to them which are in Christ Jesus" (8:1). Some have difficulty in following the train of Paul's argument as it moves out of chapter 7 into chapter 8. The subject of chapter 5 is deliverance from the penalty of sin. Chapter 6 presents sin as a tyrant from whose power the cross of Christ brings deliverance. Chapter 7 vividly depicts the civil war in the believer's heart, culminating in his cry for deliverance from sin's power. But in chapter 8 the answer apparently has reference to deliverance from sin's penalty, and it seems that the apostle has back-tracked in his argument. In reality this is not the case.

The late Archbishop Harrington C. Lees has placed us in his debt for an illuminating suggestion derived from the Greek papyri discovered in the early years of the century. Let me quote:

> One of the great debts which we owe to the modern discoveries of those who have been translating for us the Greek papyri is this: that the word "no condemnation" has a different bearing to what we often thought. The word

in the Greek though still a legal term, is *not criminal but civil*. It refers to land on which there is a legal embarrassment, a handicap, a mortgage, a restrictive covenant, a ground rent, some arrears; the dead hand of the past pressing upon the tenure of the present. The estate must be guaranteed free from that. "No drawback," says the lawyer when he makes the conveyance and passes over the estate.

So long as there is an encumbrance on the estate, the legal owner does not have full and unrestricted enjoyment of his property, since someone else has a claim on it. But to those who are "in Christ Jesus," united to Him by a living faith, there is no sort of condemnation or handicap, either civil or criminal.

Now with this fresh light on the text, it is not difficult to discern the apostle's line of argument. In chapter 7 the Christian is groaning under the pressure of past sin and failure which is cramping and blighting his present experience. The message of chapter 8 is that spiritual failure in the past need not adversely affect the present, for "there is therefore now no condemnation"—no drawback, disability, handicap, encumbrance—"to them which are in Christ Jesus." The only qualification is that we be "in Christ Jesus." Since that is our blessed privilege, this is true of us. We need no longer limp along under the crippling disabilities and handicaps of the past. There is nothing carried over from the old life whose power is not broken judicially through our union with Christ in His death and resurrection. This is the Gospel for the believer.

It is one thing to see a truth taught in the Scriptures and quite another to translate it into personal experience in the context of our own temperament and environment. What is the secret? Chapter 7 is studded with the capital "I" which occurs more than thirty times, while the Holy Spirit is mentioned only once. In chapter 8 it is the Holy Spirit who is prominent and the capital "I" occurs only twice—and even then in a joyous connection. The open secret is that deliverance from domination of sin will be ours when the capital "I" ceases to be central and the Holy Spirit is honored and obeyed. He can then mediate to us the resurrection power of Christ. The Holy Spirit is the Divine Dynamic, the Divine Stimulus. More is said about Him in this chapter than anywhere else in Scripture, with the exception of the Upper Room discourse. It is He who transforms defeat and despair into victory and delight. Chapter 8 thus presents the believer as entirely free from the hampering shackles and encumbrances of the past.

Who among us is not painfully conscious of his handicaps and disabilities in Christian living and service? We come up against them at every turn, and it is this fact which makes Paul's categorical statement of such tremendous importance to us. *"No handicap, no disability."* How glad we should be that our great High Priest shared the weaknesses of our human nature, is touched with the feeling of our infirmities, and in the gift of the Holy Spirit has made adequate provision for every drawback to which we are subject! Let us consider some of the disabilities to which the activity of the Holy Spirit is the satisfying answer.

A BIAS TOWARD SIN (8:2)

The "law of sin and death" is universally operative, giving us a fatal bias toward sin. Not one of us naturally tends toward that which is holy. "Every virtue we possess . . . is His alone." This verse reveals two opposing laws, the higher of which offsets and neutralizes the power of the lower. The power of the Divine Personality of the Holy Spirit counteracts sin's sway and leaves the believer free to fulfill the law of God of which he so heartily approves. Just as the law of life in the plant counteracts the downward pull of gravitation and allows it to express itself in flower and fruit, so the irresistible "law of the Spirit of life in Christ Jesus" neutralizes the downward bias of sin and leaves the believer free to manifest the graces and produce the fruit of the Spirit. A bias toward sin need no longer disable us.

THE DESIRES OF THE FLESH (8:5, 6)

The natural desires of our human nature, though neutral in themselves, have become debased and perverted through our racial heritage and our own indulgence in sin. "The mind of the flesh" manifests itself in unhallowed ambitions, in rivalries, in proud demeanor, in unholy longings and imaginations, in unkind and censorious speech. Even in our best moments the mind of the flesh intrudes. But when by a definite act and attitude of committal we allow the Holy Spirit to control and dominate our minds, He transforms its tastes and desires. It is for us to choose whether we will set our minds on things of the flesh or on things of the

Spirit. God cannot do that for us. But the moment we set our weak wills on God's side, the Holy Spirit immediately responds and empowers. The disabilities arising from the desires of the flesh are not final.

An Uncontrollable Heart (8:9-11)

In Melbourne, Australia, while the owners were away on vacation, a group of teen-age "rock-'n-roll" addicts commandeered their home and for two weeks staged a continuous party, leaving the home a shambles. The wrong people were in control. How fickle are our hearts, how easily drawn away from devotion to Christ by the lure of the world and the lust of the flesh! But the Holy Spirit is here revealed as the permanent Caretaker of the heart—Monitor, Censor, and Guard—and attention is drawn to His omnipotent power in this connection. He is the "Spirit of him that raised up Jesus from the dead." With this mighty Spirit in control of our hearts anything becomes possible. There is no disability of the heart where the Spirit is in control.

A Hostile Will (8:7, 13)

"The mind of the flesh is enmity against God; for it is not subject to the law of God; neither indeed can it be" (A.S.V.). We are all familiar with the manner in which our wills rise up in rebellion against the will of God. When under the impulse of sin the body asserts its desires, the will turns traitor, collaborates with it, and betrays the citadel to the enemy. Here is a grave disability, but for it there is a Divine panacea in the ministry of the Holy Spirit. "If ye through the Spirit do mortify [lead to death] the deeds of the flesh, ye shall live" (8:13). He will enable us to conduct a constant execution of that evil principle, and further will impart the will to do His good pleasure (Phil. 2:13).

AN INDEPENDENT SPIRIT (8:14)

"I *do* like to do what I like," said the little daughter of a friend. We all like to run our lives, and in most of us there is an inherent tendency to resent any authority imposed from without. Even regeneration does not eradicate the desire to "turn every one to his own way." The characteristic of the sons of God is that they are led by the Spirit of God, and *sons* here indicates not *children* but those who share the rank, character, likeness, and privilege of their Father. Independence of spirit is a mark of spiritual immaturity or decadence. Submission to the leading of the Holy Spirit is a sign of mature Christian character. The Spirit will gladly lead us when we place the reins of our lives in His hands, and will deliver us from this disability.

A TIMOROUS HEART (8:15-17)

"Ye received not the spirit of bondage again unto fear" (A.S.V.). It is not at all difficult to relapse from faith into fear, in circumstances with which some of us are familiar. All unbidden, fear tends to clutch at the heart, and before its onslaught we feel utterly impotent. Satan will endeavor to persuade us out of our sonship, as he did with Jesus, with his twice-repeated, "If thou be the

Son of God." He will attack us on our call and on our consecration at any point which will stifle confidence in God. It is here that the Holy Spirit unites with our spirit in witness that we are indeed children of God, that He did indeed call us, that our consecration was real and not counterfeit. Fear and faith are entirely incompatible, and the Holy Spirit is the Spirit of faith. When He is in control the disability of a timorous heart disappears.

A PRAYERLESS HEART (8:26, 27)

"We know not how to pray as we ought" (A.S.V.). Prayer is so complex a spiritual exercise that the ripest saint would readily subscribe to the apostle's statement. In the face of our own disinclination to pray, and our infirmities when we do overcome our reluctance, this assurance of the help of the Spirit of prayer is doubly welcome. He will assist us in the infirmities of the body. Adverse climatic, conditions lack of privacy, and difficulty in concentration, physical pain and discomfort—all come in the scope of this Divine undertaking to help our weaknesses. The Spirit of prayer will teach us to pray.

The consistent teaching of this glorious chapter is that every drawback or disability under which we may labor is more than offset by the inworking of the Holy Spirit. But one point must be underlined. *He can do in us and for us only as much as we trust Him to do.* "According to your faith be it unto you" is a principle of universal application. If we are content to continue in an unsatisfactory prayer life and do not definitely trust Him to help us in our weaknesses, we thereby shackle

His omnipotence. He will do all we trust Him to do. Do we honor Him by trusting Him fully?

During the Delhi Durbar which followed the coronation of King Edward VII, the Maharajah of Dabha had a plot of land outside Delhi allotted to him. When he went away he paid a large sum into the local treasury in order that that piece of land might be free from the burden of taxes forever. "I, the King, have rested here," he said, "therefore the land shall be free from burdens forever." And today those who are near Delhi who have no money may freely claim their place in that spot which another has paid for. They may enjoy without restriction the gift their king made to them. Our Lord Jesus too "pitched his tent" here (John 1:14), and all the blessings of which this chapter speaks have been paid for by Him. We may now enjoy them without restriction, for "there is therefore now *no condemnation* [*disability*] to them which are in Christ Jesus."

8

GOD'S PART AND OURS
IN SANCTIFICATION

Work out ... God ... worketh.
—Philippians 2:12, 13

PRESENTING SPIRITUAL TRUTH by using paradox was a favorite method of Paul's. "A paradox is an apparent contradiction," writes Dr. H.
C. Mabie, "a contradiction in terms, but not deep in
reality. Whenever in Scripture we find language
apparently self-contradictory or in apparent conflict to what is elsewhere said, we may depend on
it there is some great harmony deep down below
the surface yearning for realization."

In one passage Paul asserts that we have died,
and yet we live. He claimed to be sorrowful, yet
always rejoicing. Having nothing, he yet possessed all things; he was poor, but made many rich.
The passage before us affords another example:
"Work out your own salvation . . . for it is God
which worketh with you." It presents two essential
aspects of victorious living—what God does and
what we must do. It precludes all idea of passively
waiting with folded arms for God to intervene and
perform the miracle of deliverance and sanctification. In this, as in all else, there must be the co-

77

operation of the human with the Divine, and it is fatal to ignore either aspect. Admittedly it is difficult to determine where God's part ends and man's begins, but the Holy Spirit has been given to illumine us individually on such points.

While sanctification is by faith, it is not attained apart from man's co-operation. He is exhorted to "put off" the old man and "put on" the new man. While reckoning that "they that are Christ's have crucified the flesh with the affections and lusts" (Gal. 5:24), he is to mortify the deeds of the body. But how can we reconcile our text with Romans 4:5? "But to him that worketh not, but believeth . . . his faith is counted for righteousness." The answer is that the two ideas are complementary rather than contradictory, as we shall see.

THE EXHORTATION TO WORK

"Work out your own salvation." The strength of theological bias is evidenced in Monsignor Knox's translation of this passage: "You must work to earn your salvation in anxious fear." But the verse neither says nor means this. Paul explicitly stated that it is "your own salvation" which is to be worked out, a salvation which is already yours, not one which you are to earn by feverish and fear-ridden endeavor. He says in effect: "You have been given an estate, now go to work and develop hidden resources." Salvation is a spacious word, used of the believing man in the New Testament in three tenses. He *has been saved* from sin's guilt and penalty. He *will yet be saved* from its defiling presence. He is *now being saved* from its love and its power. Thus, past—justification; present—sanctification; and future—glorification, are involved in the expression "your own salvation."

The expression "work out" carries the idea of working out to an ultimate goal, to finish, as in a scientific or mathematical problem. The question of the believer's standing before God is never in view in the passage, nor is there room for the idea that our sanctification is something completed in a high moment of surrender to Christ. It is true that full surrender to Christ is necessary to full sanctification, but the crisis of surrender is only the initiation of the process. We have a life job on our hands. "Not as though I had already attained, either were already perfect: but I follow after" (Phil. 3:12), Paul protested. Sanctification is not automatic, the result of mere fluxion of time. The free agency of man in co-operating with God is involved. God sends sun and rain, provides soil and seed, but there would be no crop if the farmer did not plow and fertilize, sow and reap.

On one occasion that shrewd saint, George Mueller, was approached by a somnolent young man who asked his prayers that he might be able to rise in the morning for a quiet time. "Young man," he replied, "if you will get one leg out of bed I will ask the Lord to help you get the other one out." This was not only common sense but sound theology. There is a part which God alone can play in our full salvation and a part which only man can perform. But as a man in faith performs the part assigned to him, the Holy Spirit forms the transmission line along which the enabling power can flow from God, for God always responds to faith.

So then, we are to work out to a finish in terms of our own living and character the glories inherent in our own salvation. But in what spirit are we to do it? "In anxious fear," as Knox suggests? Surely not. This would be contrary to the whole spirit of the Gospel. Not in slavish fear but "in trembling and self-distrust." It has been said that in addressing men, Paul exhorts as though he were an Arminian, and in addressing God he prays as if a Calvinist, but appears to be conscious of no inconsistency in doing so. His exhortation is a warning against the peril of self-confidence in working out our own salvation. It is to be done in the spirit of dependence on the Holy Spirit, as suggested in another connection: "If ye *through the Spirit* do mortify the deeds of the body, ye shall live."

THE ENABLEMENT TO WORK

"For it is God which worketh in you." God does not exhort without providing adequate motive and incentive to encourage us to attain the highest in Christian life and character. In this clause we have a double motive presented.

The indwelling of God. We are not left to our own unaided human resources, dependent on a mere external stimulus. The eternal triune God dwells in us. "If a man love me . . . *we* will come unto him, and *make our abode* with him." "The Spirit of truth . . . shall be in you" (John 14:23, 17). There is surely sufficient incentive in this glorious fact to induce the believer to co-operate with his indwelling Guest with all His powers.

The Inworking of God. Not only does the omnipotent God dwell in the believer's heart, but is at work there, the active agent in our sanctification. "It is God which worketh [*is working*] in you," with power adequate for every need. And God's working is always effectual. How impossible it would be for man to force tons of water through solid wood! Yet every day, as the sap rises in the tree, this miracle is performed a thousand times over. With this consciousness of the Divine inworking, Paul exclaimed: "I can do all things through Christ which strengtheneth me" (Phil. 4:13). The words "all things" here do not indicate in the original that he could do "all things in the universe," but implied that he could do everything which was in the good pleasure of God for him to do. Within the sphere of God's will he enjoyed a sort of omnipotence.

THE EXTENT OF GOD'S WORKING

"To will and to do of his good pleasure." Here is another aspect of the paradox. God works within me to will and to work, and yet the willing and working are mine. But it should be noted that God does not will *instead* of me or work *instead* of me. In sanctification God and man are joined in indissoluble partnership, and all efforts to separate the respective spheres of activity are abortive. I will, but God works the will in me. I work, but God supplies the power.

The Disposition. The problem posed in Romans 7 is summarized in verse 18: "To will is present with me; but how to perform that which is good I find not." Virgil mourned: "I see a better course and I approve. But I follow the worse." He lacked the disposition to do the better thing, although with his mind he approved it. Even the regenerate man is weak so long as he tries to do the will of God by virtue of his regeneration—he finds too often that his will is paralyzed. In his translation of this verse, A. S. Way presents the activity of God as "supplying the impulse, giving you the power to resolve and the will to perform the execution of His good pleasure." We are not cast back upon our own resources. We have the benefits accruing from the death and resurrection of Christ and His gift of the Holy Spirit through whom those benefits become operative in our lives. *But I must do the choosing.* God does not impart His power or blessings apart from the active participation and co-operation of our wills. Once I put my weak will on God's side, and despite my own conscious volitional weakness choose His will, it becomes possible for the Holy Spirit to empower my vitiated will.

The Doing. Even after the right impulse has been supplied by God, giving man the power to resolve, it still remains for him to act. God cannot act for him. Sanctification is essentially positive, it does not consist merely in not doing evil things. In exercise of the new power imparted by God's Spirit he is now able to perform "his good pleasure"—the whole will of God. In himself he is no stronger, but with the Divine indwelling and inworking, he is no longer the plaything of weakness and sin.

No more apt illustration of the co-operation of man with God is recorded than that of the man with the withered hand. Try as he would, no attempted exercise of his will produced any effect on the paralyzed muscles. When our Lord commanded him to stretch out his hand, a natural reaction would have been for him to say that he had attempted to do so a thousand times, without effect. Was there any reason to expect anything different the thousand-and-first time? But faith had been kindled in the man's heart, and in response to the Lord's command, he exercized his will and to his joy the paralyzed hand responded, whole as the other. The activity of faith had released the power of God. As in the physical, so in the spiritual. "All things are possible to him that believeth."

> 'Twas most impossible of all
> That here in me sin's reign should cease.
> Yet shall it be, I know it shall,
>   'Tis certain though impossible.
>   The thing impossible shall be,
>   All things are possible to me.

9

THE NEGLECTED NINTH
BEATITUDE

It is more blessed to give than to receive.—Acts 20:35

THERE IS OFTEN a very definite connection between weakness in the spiritual life and failure
in the stewardship of money. In multitudes of lives,
bringing the whole tithe into God's storehouse has
been prelude to the opening of the windows of
Heaven in spiritual experience. Rev. R. B. Jones
of Wales maintained that the money retained in
the hands of God's people and which God owns
and claims is a most potent hindrance to a living
and strong spirituality.

In his address to the Ephesian church, Paul re-
minds his hearers of one of the few authentic sayings of our Lord not recorded in the Gospels. "Remember the words of the Lord Jesus . . . It is more
blessed to give than to receive" (Acts 20:35). Not
without purpose did the Holy Spirit preserve this
ninth beatitude which underscores the superior
blessedness of liberality. Elsewhere he refers to
Christian giving as a neglected grace. "See that
ye abound in this grace also," he urges the Corinthian Christians (II Cor. 8:7). Can we affirm that

we have both exhibited this grace and experienced this beatitude?

THE ACID TEST

Money is one of the acid tests of character and a surprising amount of space is given to it in Scripture. One teacher asserted that one verse in six in the Synoptic Gospels has to do with money, either directly or indirectly. In sixteen out of thirty-eight of our Lord's parables, the subject of money is involved. Whether a man is rich or poor, observe his reaction to his possessions and you have a revealing index to his character. Like many since, the rich young man of Mark's Gospel became the abject slave of his great possessions. Instead of his having them, they held him so securely that he chose to lose his soul rather than sacrifice the temporal advantage they conferred. To use our money without parsimony and yet avoid extravagance is no mean achievement. It requires that fine spiritual balance —*sophrosune*—which was so highly esteemed among the Greeks and was set before the believers in Rome by Paul as a greatly desired goal (Rom. 12:3).

Much of our thinking concerning money and its stewardship is definitely subscriptural. The phrase "his lord's money" (Matt. 25:18) is deeply significant. The basic question is not how much of *our money* we shall give to God, but how much of *God's money* we shall retain for ourselves. The correct answer to that question will lead infallibly to the experience of the beatitude of which our Lord spoke. Both money and the power to earn it are a gift and a stewardship from God. We are not owners but only trustees of our possessions and must render an account of our stewardship. One of the most scathing indictments in Scripture is of the Jews of Malachi's day, who picked the pockets of God Himself by keeping their choicest possessions for themselves, while offering Him the worthless refuse (Mal. 3:8, 9). "Will a man rob God? . . . Ye have robbed me," are the words of Jehovah. But such is the grace of God that He immediately follows His indictment with a promise of overflowering blessing if the tithe is paid (v. 10). Unfortunately such hypocrisy is not peculiar to the time of Malachi. Calvin lamented in his day that the heathen contributed more to their gods to express their superstitions than Christian people were giving to the cause of Christ to express their love, and the same is true of our times. But so, thank God, is the promise of outpoured blessing when His conditions are fulfilled.

LAW OF THE TITHE

From the dawn of history giving of tithes was common practice (Gen. 14:20). The consecration of tithes was as customary with Roman, Greek, and Arabian as with the Jew. It is true the practice received Divine sanction at Sinai, but we must remember that the law of the tithe antedated the law of Moses by four hundred years. To the Jew it was an inescapable obligation and in addition he gave thank-offerings and alms. The devout Jew customarily gave one-fifth of his income to God and to charitable purposes.

There are some who contend that since Christians are "not under law but under grace," the law of the tithe has been abrogated for them. But surely we do not desire to become antinominian in the matter of Christian liberality. Are we not still "under law to Christ" with His higher law of love? Shall we take advantage of grace to reduce our giving below the level of the Jew under law? Little wonder Chrysostom exclaimed concerning such an attitude: "Oh, what a shame that what was no great matter among the Jews should be pretended to be such among Christians!" Did not our Lord, as a devout Jew, give more than a tenth into His Father's treasury, and did He not leave us an example that we should follow His steps?

Admittedly, tithing is nowhere specifically commanded in the New Testament, since that is not the genius of God's method under grace. "I speak not by commandment" were Paul's words used in this very context (II Cor. 8:8). He knew that a lavish hand without a loving heart was spiritually valueless. Only the overflowing love and grace of Christ can make a selfish heart unselfish. In the warm glow of their Pentecostal love, the early disciples "sold their possessions and goods, and parted to every man as he had need." To them sacrificial giving to God was a spiritual luxury, not an irksome duty to be evaded if at all possible. Even Jacob the swindler gave his tithe, Zacchaeus the extortioner one-half, and the penurious widow "all her living."

MODEL STEWARDSHIP

The model of Christian stewardship held up to the rich and richly gifted but ungenerous Corinthian church was the poverty-stricken church in

Macedonia (II Cor. 8:1-5). Remarkable people were these Macedonians. In striking contrast to their deep poverty and affliction shone the riches of their abounding liberality (v. 2). Despite their limited resources—for they were pioneer settlers —they did not shrink from giving beyond their ability and to the point of real sacrifice (v. 3). They did not wait to be urged but pleaded for the privilege of giving (vv. 3, 4). "With earnest entreaty they implored me." Their offering of hard-won money was preceded by the more costly surrender of their very selves (v. 5). The spirit of liberality which they evinced proved provocative (II Cor. 9:2) and inspired Paul to place before the church of all ages the supreme example of giving—that of our Lord who gladly impoverished Himself for our enrichment (v. 9). Would that we all, whether we have much or little, gave to the Lord with such hilarious and uncalculating abandon!

The intrinsic value of any act is, of course, determined by its inspiring motive. The condition of the donor's heart is all-important. If we give merely or mainly in order to secure God's blessing on our business or professional advancement or even to secure personal spiritual blessing, we thereby neutralize our gift. Only those gifts which have their birth in a heart of love to Christ are acceptable to God. Robert G. LeTourneau, himself a faithful steward, wisely remarked, "If you give because it pays, then it won't pay." Our Lord assessed the value of the widow's gift not so much by its quantity as by the quality of the devotion which prompted her to give, not one-tenth but "all her living." The Divine measuring rod is not the monetary value of the gift but the sacrifice involved—not the amount given but the amount remaining. If we give only what we can spare without affecting our comfort, this is not Christian giving at all.

It is only to be expected that the impulse to liberality should be challenged in a variety of ways by the ever-vigilant Enemy. He will endeavor to dry up the fountains of generosity in the soul by suggesting postponement until some time when it will be easier or more convenient. It is extremely unlikely that such a time will ever come. The stifling of a generous impulse today makes it easier to do the same tomorrow. Another mode of attack is to freeze the assets of the generous man so that he has no liquid cash to give. Expanding the business demands reinvestment of every available dollar, or more money must be put in to save existing investments. How familiar has the pattern become! When income increases, the Tempter encourages a proportionate increase in the standard of living which swallows up the increase and no more is available for giving than before. It was far different with John Wesley. When earning thirty pounds a year he lived on twenty-six pounds, and gave four pounds to God. When his income doubled, he continued to live on twenty-six pounds but gave thirty-four pounds to the Lord. Little wonder that God entrusted him in such abundant measure with the true spiritual riches.

Extra-Corpus Benevolence

Another stratagem of the adversary is to short-circuit liberality by what the late A. J. Gordon aptly styled *extra-corpus benevolence*—the postponement of generosity until after death. "Why is it," he asks, "that so many Christians make death their executor, leaving thousands and millions to be dispensed by his bony fingers? If they die, their wealth can stay behind; their covetousness can survive and reap postmortem usury! It is doubtless wise to make such modest provision for our dependents as we are able, but surely it cannot be termed Christian generosity when a man waits until death shakes religious and charitable legacies from his pockets. Let us give all we can during our lifetime and have the joy of seeing our money working for God. God promises a reward for 'deeds done *in* the body,' not out of it. His command is unequivocally clear to all who are willing to hear. 'Lay not up for yourselves treasures upon earth ... Lay up for yourselves treasures in heaven' (Matt. 6:19, 20). To be generous with God from right motives brings its reward here as well as hereafter."

The harvest we reap in the coming day will be in exact proportion to our sowing, for "he which soweth sparingly shall reap also sparingly; and he which soweth bountifully shall reap also bountifully" (II Cor. 9:6). There is an unfailing law of recompense which operates in favor of the liberal soul. "Give, and it shall be given unto you; good measure, pressed down, and shaken together, and running over . . . . For with the same measure that

ye mete withal, it shall be measured to you again"
(Luke 6:38). The converse is also true. "There is
that withholdeth more than is meet, and it tend-
eth to poverty" (Prov. 11:24). It could be a
salutary and wholesome exercise to examine our
past stewardship in the light of Calvary and the
judgment seat of Christ, and to make any amend-
ment the Spirit of God might suggest.

10

SOME GUIDING PRINCIPLES
OF CONDUCT

Under ... law to Christ.—I Corinthians 9:21

ALL OF US, but perhaps more particularly younger Christians, are perplexed at times concerning the righteousness or otherwise of a course of action we propose to follow. "Would it be right for me as a Christian to do this, or to go there?" is a question to which we earnestly desire to find an authoritative and satisfying answer. How can it be found? Many have been brought up under a series of taboos, especially on questions of worldliness, and have often yielded to the convictions of others of which they themselves are not fully convinced.

Such an attitude is not always conducive to a virile and healthy spiritual experience since it is one derived largely at secondhand. We must by diligent study of the Scriptures, by thought and prayer, arrive at our own convictions and not weakly adopt those inherited from others.

But having said that, we should guard against the idea that there is no place for taboos and prohibitions in the Christian life. They are plentifully found in both Old and New Testaments— the Ten Commandments, for example. If it be objected that we are "not under law but under grace," and that the restrictions of the law do not apply to Christians, the answer is that nine out of ten commandments in the Decalogue are reiterated in the New Testament, where their application is greatly widened. Murder in the act is traced to hatred in the heart. It is true that we are no longer "under the law" as a way of justification but we are "under . . . law to Christ" as a new way of life. Paul is as free with his prohibitions as with his exhortations. "Put off," "abstain," "lay aside" are characteristic of his letters.

The Bible does not legislate in detail for every matter of conduct which might arise, but it does enumerate clear principles which, correctly applied, cover every conceivable case. If God did not thus give clear guidance how can we then be held responsible for failure to do His will? It is the genius of New Testament Christianity to lay down clear guiding principles rather than to impose a set of taboos, a system of rules and regulations, for God delights to deal with His people as adult sons rather than as children under a tutor. Since this is the case, in reading the Scriptures we should constantly ask, "What are the spiritual principles propounded in this passage?"

If we are to receive guidance, absolute sincerity of purpose is essential, for God undertakes to reveal His will only to the one who is prepared to do it. There must be a complete willingness to accept the dictum of the Bible as final in all matters of faith and practice. To approach a doubtful matter with such questions as "Where is the harm in it?" or "Others do it, why not I?" is to indicate that it has been prejudged and it is not so much guidance which is sought as sanction. The mind is almost made up already. "If any man willeth to do his will, he shall know . . . " (John 7:17) is a principle of universal application. Where there is a genuine purpose to do God's will as soon as He reveals it, the seeker will not remain long in darkness. But conversely, unwillingness to do God's will effectively excludes the light of Divine guidance.

Six Eliminating Questions

To ask and answer the following positive questions will automatically dispose of many problems concerning doubtful things.

Will it bring glory to God? "Whatsoever ye do, do all to the glory of God" (I Cor. 10:31). If the chief end of man is to glorify God, this should be our first test and chief concern. If the proposed course terminates on self and does not bring glory to God, it is something which can well be laid aside.

Is it profitable? Will it help me in my Christian life, my witness, my service? "All things are lawful for me, but all things are not expedient: all things are lawful for me, but all things edify not" (I Cor. 10:23). Will it tend to make my life more profitable to God and to my fellow man?

Does it edify? Does it build me up in my Christian character and will it help me to build up the church of God? "For edification, and not for your destruction" (II Cor. 10:8). God's supreme interest is centered in His church and we should share His concern for its upbuilding.

Does it tend to enslave? "All things are lawful for me; but I will not be brought under the power of any" (I Cor. 6:12, A.S.V.). Even things in themselves lawful can become our master and get out of proportion. They can so demand our attention that we neglect other things of more importance. For example, secular reading can so enslave a reader that it vitiates his appetite for the reading of the Word of God and spiritual books. Such a condition must be jealously guarded against by strict self-discipline, both as to the quality and the quantity of our secular reading.

Will it strengthen me against temptation? It is of little avail for us to pray, "Lead us not into temptation," if we voluntarily go where we will be exposed to temptation. It is one thing for a Salvation Army officer to enter a tavern to sell his *War Cry* but quite another for a young man to go in to "celebrate" with his friends. Any place or practice which tends to make sin less sinful is to be shunned.

Is it characteristic of the world or of the Father? "For all that is in the world, the lust of the flesh, the lust of the eyes, and the pride of life, is not of the Father, but is of the world" (I John 2:16). If the proposed course of action is more characteristic of the world, our course is clear for "if any man love the world, the love of the Father is not in him" (I John 2:15). The world and the things that are in the world are not to be the dominating objects of our affection.

But there are many relationships, pleasures, and activities which, while not sins, could be termed "weights," for they impede progress in the heavenly race and should therefore be laid aside. Dr. G. Campbell Morgan points out that "the things which hinder are not necessarily low or vulgar. They may be in themselves noble things, intellectual things, beautiful things. But if our participation in any of these dims our vision of the ultimate goal in the purpose of God, holds us in our running, makes our going less determined and steady, they become weights and hinder."

Let us now consider six principles concerning questionable conduct enunciated by Paul under the inspiration of the Holy Spirit. He dealt with some problems faced by the Roman Christians which are similar to the difficulties we encounter today.

SIX GUIDING PRINCIPLES

Every important spiritual truth and doctrine is treated fully in at least one extended passage in the Scriptures. The subject of doubtful things is fully treated in Romans 14, in which Paul lays down the following principles.

Liberty of judgment. "Let not him that eateth [meat] despise him that eateth not [i.e., the vegetarian]; and let not him which eateth not judge him that eateth" (Rom. 14:2). The point at issue was whether or not it was permissable for a Christian to eat meat offered to idols. Well-taught believers, realizing that an idol was nothing at all, felt quite free to eat such meat; but to some less instructed it was a cause of stumbling, so they eschewed eating meat at all. Here was a potential cause for friction, where no vital doctrine was at stake, so Paul exhorts an attitude of tolerance. Within the Christian church there is to be room for genuine difference of opinion. We are to recognize and maintain the right of our brother to hold opinions opposed to our own.

Right of personal conviction. "Let every man be fully persuaded in his own mind" (Rom. 14:5). It is very easy for us, chameleonlike, to take our theological color from the people by whom we are surrounded. The result is that we are as likely to be swayed by mere theological prejudice as by the Word of God. Paul's exhortation is that we should be fully persuaded in our own mind concerning the matter under review and not allow our conduct to be dictated by someone else, however admirable their character and qualification. The decision must be our own decision, for we alone are responsible for our actions.

Accountability to God alone. It is "to his own master he standeth or falleth" (14:4). It is to God alone that we are responsible, for "every one of us shall give account of himself to God" (14:12). While recognizing that we are members of a society in which we have responsibility, Paul emphasizes that our final accountability is to God alone. Since One is our Master, Christ, anyone else—be he pope or bishop or minister—who arrogates to himself a sovereignty over our actions is infringing the "crown rights of the Redeemer." The fact that "we must all appear before the judgment seat of Christ" will deeply influence the conduct of all who sincerely wish to do the will of God.

Absence of censoriousness when others differ. "But why dost thou judge thy brother? or why dost thou set at nought thy brother?" (14:10). "Let us not therefore judge one another any more" (14: 13). "Who art thou that judgest another man's servant? to his own master he standeth or falleth" (14:4). It is not our prerogative to judge and criticize our brother's actions. That is the right of God alone, and further, we shall all be judged one day, not by one another, but "before the judgment seat of Christ" (14:10). We must be careful that "no man put a stumblingblock or an occasion to fall in his brother's way" (14:13). We are to attribute to our brother the same degree of sincerity in his actions as we would wish him to attribute to us.

Abstinence in the interests of others. "Love worketh no ill to his neighbor" (13:10). "It is good not to eat flesh, nor to drink wine, nor to do anything whereby thy brother stumbleth" (14:21, A.S.V.). "We bear all things, that we may cause no hindrance to the gospel of Christ" (I Cor. 9: 12, A.S.V.). The Christian is not to live for his own pleasure alone, but is ever to bear in mind the effect his conduct may have on his weaker brother. The freedom of many a moderate drinker has proved the undoing of a weaker man who did not have the same measure of control of his appetite. We must watch lest our freedom prove a stumbling stone to our brother. It is for us, for Christ's sake, to voluntarily forego our legitimate enjoyment for the sake of our weaker brother. "We then that are strong ought to bear the infirmities of the weak, and not to please ourselves" (15:1).

Abstinence from things doubtful. "He that doubteth is condemned . . . because . . . whatsoever is not of faith is sin" (14:23, A.S.V.). The very fact that we have doubts raises the presumption that the matter is questionable. Any action we take should carry with it the positive assurance of faith. The presence of doubt is a call to defer action until by prayer and diligent searching of the Scriptures we arrive at a conviction as to what we should do. In this as in all others, we never lose if we give to God the benefit of any doubt. It may be, however, that we have a "weak" conscience on the matter which needs to be educated by the Word of God. It is quite possible through tradition or prejudice to have doubts about what the Bible does not condemn.

We must not overlook the gracious ministry of the Holy Spirit whose work it is to guide us into all truth. "The leadership and discipline of the Holy Spirit through the moral standards of the Word of God; this is the true basis of moral Christian living," says C. B. Eavey. "It is morality without legalism, not contrary to the eternal law of God, but in the spirit of the law. True morality . . . must be inward. The Holy Spirit makes the precepts of the law live in the heart and control the motives of the heart. When the leading and disciplining of the Holy Spirit are sincerely accepted and wholly followed, there is a refined sensitivity that lifts ethical practice above all legalism."

PART TWO

PROBLEMS IN CHRISTIAN SERVICE

11

CONDITIONS OF SPIRITUAL LEADERSHIP

He that is chief . . . doth serve.—Luke 22:26

And there was also a strife among them, which of them should be accounted the greatest. And he said unto them, The kings of the Gentiles exercise lordship over them: and they that exercise authority upon them are called benefactors. But ye shall not be so: but he that is greatest among you, let him be as the younger; and he that is chief, as he that doth serve. For whether is greater, he that sitteth at meat, or he that serveth? is not he that sitteth at meat? but I am among you as he that serveth. —Luke 22:24-27

COURSES IN LEADERSHIP are the order of the day, a tacit admission that leaders are in short supply. The fact is that there has always been a dearth of leaders of the right caliber, whether it be in secular or in sacred realms. In the Scriptures God is frequently represented as searching for a man of a certain type. "The Lord hath sought him a man after his own heart" (I Sam. 13:14). "I beheld, and, lo, there was no man" (Jer. 4:25). "Run ye to and fro through the streets of Jerusalem, and see . . . if ye can find a man . . . that executeth judgment, that seeketh the truth; and I will pardon it" (Jer. 5:1). "I sought a man . . . that should . . . stand in the gap" (Ezek. 22:30, A.S.V.). And when He does discover a man who conforms to His spiritual requirements—a John Wesley, a William Booth, a Hudson Taylor, a Billy Graham—despite their obvious limitations and shortcomings, it seems as though there is no limit to what He will do for and through them.

One of the greatest needs of the church today is for authoritative, spiritual, and sacrificial leadership. Authoritative, because people love to be led by one who knows where he is going and who inspires their confidence. Spiritual, because a leadership which is carnal and explainable in terms of the natural, be it ever so competent, can result only in sterility and spiritual bankruptcy. Sacrificial, because it is modeled on the life of One who gave Himself a sacrifice for the whole world, and who stated that the path to leadership was by the lonely road to sacrificial service.

Its Nature

The nature of true spiritual leadership is indicated in a sentence from the pen of the late Dr. S. M. Zwemer: "There was never a world in greater need of men and women who know the way, and can keep ahead and draw others to follow." If we are to become leaders it will be because we can show the way to others, the way which we have successfully trodden ourselves. We can lead others only so far as we ourselves have gone, and we are leaders only to the extent that we inspire others to follow us. Because he himself has qualified, a leader can secure the co-operation of others in achieving some work for God.

His leadership will not be so much the result of the force of his own personality, potent though that may be, as of the welcomed domination of that personality by the Holy Spirit. Because of the Spirit's unhindered operation, he possesses a spiritual authority greater than that of his followers. While the power of his influence is not altogether independent of his natural endowments, it cannot be explained on that level alone, for in many things natural and spiritual leadership are very diverse. There is, however, much we can learn from the principles which govern even natural leadership.

In *Operation Victory,* Field Marshal Montgomery enunciates seven ingredients of military leadership which are equally applicable to the spiritual leader:

He should be able to sit back and avoid getting immersed in detail.

He must not be petty.

He must not be pompous.

He must be a good picker of men.

He should trust those under him and let them get on with their job without interference.

He must have the power of clear decision.

He should inspire confidence.

Few Christian leaders had greater experience over a long period in selecting and training leaders than the late John R. Mott, whose tests for leadership follow:

Does he do little things well?

Has he learned the meaning of priorities?

How does he use his leisure?

Has he intensity?

Has he learned to take advantage of momentum?

Has he the power of growth?

What is his attitude to discouragements?

How does he face impossible situations?

What are his weakest points?

POWER OF INFLUENCE

Since leadership is essentially the power of one man to influence others, it may be out of place to consider here the almost limitless possibilities of a single life. "None of us liveth to himself, and no man dieth to himself" (Rom. 14:7). Both Scripture and experience affirm that none of us can be neutral either morally or spiritually. We leave on the lives which come within the range of our influence an indelible impress for good or ill. Dr. John Geddie went to Aneityuin in 1848, remaining there twenty-four years. On the tablet erected to his memory are these words: "When he landed in 1848 there were no Christians; when he left in 1872, there were no heathen."

The following striking contrast between the influence for good or ill of two American families has been preserved for us by Dr. Winship:

"The father of Jonathan Edwards was a minister and his mother was the daughter of a clergyman. Among their descendants were fourteen presidents of colleges, more than one hundred college professors, more than one hundred lawyers, thirty judges, sixty physicians, more than a hundred clergymen, missionaries and theology professors, and about sixty authors. There is scarcely any great American industry that has not had one of his family among its chief promoters. Such is the product of one American Christian family, reared under the most favorable conditions. The contrast is presented in the Jukes family, which could not be made to study and would not work, and is said to have cost the state of New York a million dollars. Their entire record is one of pauperism and crime, insanity and imbecility. Among their twelve hundred known descendants, three hundred ten were professional paupers, four hundred forty were physically wrecked by their own wickedness, sixty were habitual thieves, one hundred thirty were convicted criminals, fifty-five were victims of impurity, only twenty learned a trade (and ten of these learned it in a state prison), and this notorious family produced seven murderers."

QUALIFICATIONS

There is a military organization known as "Officers' Selection and Appraisal Center," where men are tested for leadership. When a man arrives at OSAC, be he private or captain, he becomes just a number. All ranks are leveled. Each washes dishes and shines shoes like the other. What is observed is not knowledge or proficiency, but reaction to the unexpected, to uncongenial conditions or criticism, or to crisis. Each man is constantly interviewed scrutinized, tested, to discern his caliber for leadership. God too has his OSAC, and often-times all unknown to us we disqualify ourselves for responsible service by our reactions to the tests to which He subjects us.

For what qualities of character, then, is God looking in potential leaders?

The supremely important characteristic is true *spirituality*. "He that is spiritual judgeth [discerneth] all things," affirms Paul (I Cor. 2:15). In reference to ministry to an erring brother, Paul admonished the Galatian leaders: "Ye which are spiritual restore such an one in the spirit of meekness" (Gal. 6:1). Even for positions of minor leadership, the early church demanded "men . . . full of the Holy Ghost and wisdom" (Acts 6:3). Spirituality is the manifestation in the life of the consecrated believer of the power and influence of the Holy Spirit. To be filled with the Spirit is to be controlled by the Spirit. In his lexicon Thayer says: "That which takes possession of the mind is said to fill it." Luke 5:26 records that the disciples were "filled with fear"; fear possessed their minds. John 16:6 records that when Jesus told them of His impending departure, His disciples were filled with sorrow; sorrow controlled their minds. Exactly the same word occurs in "be filled with the Spirit" (Eph. 5:18). A spiritual man is one whose mind and heart and personality are possessed and controlled by the Holy Spirit. Every Spirit-filled man is to some degree a spiritual leader.

He will be a man of deep *humility*. This quality is neither required nor coveted in politics or commerce, but it is essential in true spiritual leadership. In the simple words at the head of this chapter the Master gave His conception of the pathway to leadership. The Gentile kings might be pompous, but the man who is great in the kingdom of Heaven will be humble like his Master. This man will prefer the pathway of hidden sacrificial service to the adulation of the crowd. "Whosoever will be great among you, let him be your minister; and whosoever will be chief among you, let him be your servant" (Matt. 20:26, 27). He will be able to lead people only insofar as he serves and helps them. The secret which made John the Baptist greatest of those born of women is to be found in his revealing declaration: "He [Christ] must increase, but I must decrease" (John 3:30).

The humility of the leader, as his spirituality, will be an ever-increasing quality. It is instructive to note Paul's growth in this grace as the years went by. Early in his ministry, as he reviewed his unsavory past, he acknowledged: "I am the least of the apostles, that I am not meet to be called an apostle" (I Cor. 15:9). Sometime later he volunteered: I "am less than the least of all saints" (Eph. 3:8). As his life was drawing to a close he mourned: I am the chief of sinners (I Tim. 1:15).

His life will be characterized by *self-discipline*. The words *discipline* and *disciple* come from the same root. Only the disciplined person knows true discipleship, to say nothing of leadership. The leader will work while others waste time, pray while others play, study while others sleep. He will observe a soldierly discipline in dress and diet, that he might wage a good warfare. He will do the unpleasant task or the hidden duty which others avoid because it evokes no applause and wins no appreciation.

He will not rebel at a discipline imposed from without. There are multitudes who are willing to lead but who are not willing to obey. Some boys were playing at war. When a passer-by inquired why they were so quiet, one boy replied, "We are all generals. We can't get anyone to do the fighting." A good leader must first prove himself a good and loyal follower of those over him in the Lord. He knows how to be an individual without being individualistic. Because he himself is strongly disciplined, others will accept his strong discipline. His constant prayer is:

> From subtle love of softening things,
> From easy choices, weakenings,
> (Not thus are spirits fortified,
> Not this way went the Crucified)
> From all that dims Thy Calvary,
> O Lamb of God, deliver me.
>
> —AMY CARMICHAEL

He will be a man of *vision*. The old prophets were called seers because they had a keener spiritual perception than their contemporaries. The spiritual leader sees things clearly as in the light of eternity. "Vision is more than sight, or even insight. It is to see the invisible." All the Biblical characters who made an indelible impression on their own generation possessed this quality in marked degree. Because the leader sees farther than his followers, he will set the standard high, though this may not always tend to popularity. He will endeavor to hold them to the highest, and because he sees the ultimate so clearly, he will not permit them to sacrifice the ultimate for the immediate.

Finally, he will be a man of swift and clear *decision*. Once sure of the will of God he will go into immediate action, regardless of consequences. "A leader is a man who can burn his bridges behind him." Circumstances will not frustrate him, nor difficulties deter. Because his aim is single and his motive pure, his decisions are not complex and he does not vacillate.

In one of his last messages before his death in an airplane crash, Fred Mitchell, of the China Inland Mission, said: "It is the quality of leaders that they can bear to be sat on, absorb shocks, act as a buffer, bear being much plagued. . . . Moses put up with the complaints and the waywardness and revolt of the people. He pursued a steady course, enduring as seeing Him who is invisible. The wear and tear and the continual friction and trials which come to the servants of God are a great test of character."

How Attained

Leaders are not made by mere election or appointment. Spiritual authority cannot be conferred by bishops or boards. Spiritual leaders seldom seek place or position. It usually comes unsought to those who by spirituality, character, and ability have proved themselves worthy of it. They are men who have mastered Jehovah's counsel to Baruch: "Seekest thou great things for thyself? seek them not" (Jer. 45:5).

Samuel Logan Brengle, himself a man of singular spiritual power, set forth in oft-quoted words the road to spiritual authority. "It is not won by promotion, but by many tears and confessions of sin, and humblings and heartsearchings and self-surrender; a courageous sacrifice of every idol, a bold uncomplaining and uncompromising embracing of the cross. It is not gained by seeking great things for ourselves, but like Paul, in counting those things which were gain, loss for Christ. That is a great price, but it must be paid by him who would be a real leader."

Not all who seek leadership are prepared to pay such an exacting price. But God's conditions must be complied with in secret before He will honor a man in public.

WARNINGS

The possession of this spiritual authority will not render a man infallible. Because he is human and compassed with infirmity, he will still be prone to make mistakes. But a genuine mistake is not necessarily sin. It is better to have made an honest mistake than to have attempted nothing for God. Even apostles appeared at times to make mistakes which God subsequently overruled.

The spiritual leader is not rendered immune from the operation of natural laws. If he breaks physical laws, he will pay the physical penalty. Many of the holiest and ablest men have temporarily broken under the almost intolerable burdens they carried. At the end of his life, John Knox, the great Scottish reformer, lost heart, withdrew from public life, and wrote despairingly: "Lord Jesus, receive my spirit and put an end to this miserable life, for justice and truth are not to be found among the sons of men. John Knox, with deliberate mind, to his God." It is not without its comfort that the two men who conversed with the Lord on the Mount of Transfiguration both broke under the strain of their ministry and prayed that they might die.

Spiritual leadership once bestowed is not automatically retained. Samson enjoyed the unlimited power of the Spirit for a long time, and even when he was trifling with the secret of his power. But at last his sin caught up with him. "And he wist not that the Lord was departed from him" (Judges 16:20). Paul entertained no illusions on this score and in his letter to the Corinthians tells them of his fear of being disapproved at the last (I Cor. 9:27).

It appears that God deals more stringently with the sins of a leader than with those of his followers. Since the very nature of his responsibilities keeps him constantly in the public eye as the representative of God, God's honor is involved in his. For forty years Moses was the focal center of Israel's national and religious life. All eyes were on him. All his actions were public actions and hence the severity of God's dealing with a sin which, at first blush, did not appear so serious.

But there is a blessed complementary truth. Although God deals severely with the erring leader, He also deals severely with those who would challenge the authority of the leader He has endorsed. When the sons of Korah gathered together against Moses and said: "Ye take too much upon you . . . wherefore then lift ye up yourselves above the congregation of the Lord?" (Num. 16:3), the divine vindication was swift. "And the earth opened her mouth, and swallowed them up" (Num. 16: 32). Even when Miriam, Moses' older sister, criticized him for his choice of a wife, God smote her with leprosy which was healed only at Moses' intercession. A God-appointed spiritual leader is perfectly safe when, and only when, he walks humbly with his God, for God is very jealous of the authority of those whom He has endorsed.

It remains to be said that leadership often involves loneliness, especially in the work of the kingdom of God. The mental anguish sometimes involved in making a difficult or unpopular decision can be fully known only by those called upon to do it.

12

GOD-SANCTIONED AMBITION

Enlarge my coast.

And Jabez was more honorable than his
brethren: and his mother called his name Jabez,
saying, Because I bare him with sorrow. And
Jabez called on the God of Israel, saying, Oh
that thou wouldest bless me indeed, and enlarge my coast, and that thine hand might be
with me, and that thou wouldest keep me
from evil, that it may not grieve me! And
God granted him that which he requested.
—I Chronicles 4:9, 10

CROMWELL, I CHARGE THEE, fling away ambition: by that sin fell the angels." When
Shakespeare put these words into the mouth of one
of his characters, Cardinal Wolsey, was he giving
advice which accords with the teaching of Scripture? Is ambition necessarily a base and selfish
quality? Is it indeed the "last infirmity of noble
minds"?

The Bible appears to teach that there is an ambition which warrants these strictures, but also that
there is an ambition which is worthy and to be
cherished. In essence, any ambition which centers
around and terminates upon oneself is unworthy,

while an ambition which has the glory of God as its center is not only legitimate but positively praiseworthy.

A MASTER AMBITION

Many fail of worth-while achievement simply because they have no master ambition, no dominating purpose to unify their lives. They live haphazardly and not like Paul, who said, "This one thing I do."

The story is told of the father of the famous Webster brothers, who found the boys lounging around listlessly. "What are you doing, Ezekiel?" he demanded. "Doing nothing." "And what are you doing, Daniel?" "Helping Zeke, sir."

If we are to achieve a worth-while ambition it will require such a wholehearted abandonment as the orator Demosthenes displayed in pursuit of oratorical power. Dr. A. T. Pierson tells that when Demosthenes first spoke in public he was hissed off the platform. His voice was harsh and weak and his appearance unprepossessing. He determined that his fellow citizens would yet hang on his words, and to this end he gave himself day and night to elocution. He shaved half his head so that he would not be drawn into the involvements of society life. To overcome a stammer he recited with pebbles in his mouth. He matched his orations with the thunders of the Aegean Sea that his voice might gain in volume. An ugly hitching of the shoulder he corrected by standing beneath a suspended sword. He corrected any facial distortions he practiced in front of a mirror. It is not surprising that when he next appeared in public, he moved the nation. He was speaking with another orator on a matter of vital moment to the nation. When his companion concluded his speech the crowd said, "What marvelous oratory!" But when Demosthenes reached his peroration they cried with one voice, "Let us go and fight Philip!"

Worldly ambition expresses itself in three main directions: to build a reputation, to amass wealth, to wield power, but its fatal flaw is that its center is self and not God. This ambition does not ennoble: it engenders jealousy and envy. It is impatient of the consideration due to others and will go to all lengths to achieve its end. It drives the "successful" businessman to crush ruthlessly his weaker and more scrupulous competitor. But how tawdry and unsubstantial are its rewards and how trivial its achievements when viewed in the light of eternity! The ambition of a Napoleon or a Hitler brought them momentary glory, but with its eternal shame. Such an ambition as this is the antithesis of the spirit of the cross of Christ.

An Unworthy Ambition

It is possible to nurse an unworthy ambition in religious as well as in worldly associations. Before their transforming experience at Pentecost, two of our Lord's intimates, James and John, used their doting mother in an endeavor to gain them a preferment over their ten brethren. They stooped to petty intrigue to exclude the other claimants to the places of supreme privilege in Christ's kingdom. Even the Last Supper was not too sacred an occasion to be marred by their selfish strife. Nor were the ten free from the same unworthy ambition, else why were they so indignant with James and John for forestalling them? They had yet to learn, and by very bitter experience, that the lowliest is the greatest in Christ's kingdom; but they did master the lesson.

The ambition which God sanctions is far otherwise. The true disciple of Christ lives by an entirely different scale of values. A God-approved ambition must be pure and noble, tinged with self-abnegation and self-sacrifice. The disciple recognizes that he belongs to Christ—body, intellect, emotions, and will—and therefore any honor which may come to him belongs to his Master. Like his Lord, he cherishes the ambition to give rather than to receive, to serve rather than to be served, to use his time and talents for his Master rather than debase them in pursuit of self-aggrandizement.

The Determining Motive

It is the underlying motive which determines the character of ambition and renders it laudable or unworthy. "Seekest thou great things *for thyself?* seek them not," was God's message to Baruch (Jer. 45:5). In His memorable Sermon on the Mount Christ counseled: "Lay not up *for yourselves* treasures upon earth" (Matt. 6:19). The wrong lies not in the ambition itself but in its inspiring motive. An intensely ambitious man himself, Paul encouraged others to aim high by citing himself as an example. "I press toward the mark for the prize" (Phil. 3:14). "So run, that ye may obtain" (I Cor. 9:24). "Study to show thyself approved unto God, a workman that needeth not to be ashamed" (II Tim. 2:15). Three of Paul's own unusual ambitions appear—some quite incidentally—in his epistles: to be "well-pleasing to God" (Phil. 4:18); "to be quiet," the quiet of inner repose, not of inertia (I Thess. 4:11); and "to preach the gospel, not where Christ was named" (Rom. 15:20). All his ambitions found their center in Christ, "that in all things *he* might have the pre-eminence" (Col. 1:18).

David Brainerd was so consumed with ambition to glorify Christ by winning souls for His kingdom that he wrote in his diary: "I cared not where or how I lived, or what hardships I endured so that I could but gain souls for Christ. While I was asleep I dreamt of such things, and when I waked the first thing I thought of was winning souls to Christ."

The supreme ambition of George Whitefield found expression in this tremendous sentence: "If God did not give me souls, I believe I would die."

Here then is the measuring rod for an ambition which is legitimate for the Christian. Is its supreme objective the glory of God and not the glory of the disciple? Will its fulfillment make the disciple more useful in Christ's service and a greater blessing to his fellow men? Theodore Monod compressed it into this motto: "All in Christ, by the Holy Spirit, for the glory of God."

One of the great Bible examples of holy ambition is found in the passage at the head of this chapter. This brief paragraph affords a remarkable insight into the character and ambitions of the one man whom God had singled out from among all his contemporaries for honorable mention. It is a remarkable thumbnail sketch which lays bare the ambition which caused him to become "more honorable than his brethren." Its very setting, an oasis in the wilderness of the dead, would indicate the importance which God attached to his attainments. When God troubles to preserve the epitaph of one man out of millions and gives it in such concise and meaningful language, we can be certain that it will repay detailed study.

Before passing to the other subject of his ambition, two lessons from the life of Jabez are worthy of note.

There is no need for *obscurity to overshadow a life*. Only the bare essentials relevant to the divine purpose are contained in the epitaph of Jabez. No indication is given that he was wealthy, gifted, or even popular—only that he became more honorable than his brethren, and his contemporaries too, for of him alone does God preserve a record for posterity. Church history teaches that God sometimes takes up obscure men or women and uses them to an extraordinary degree while passing by people of much greater gift. Jabez sprang out of obscurity into agelong prominence because of his secret prayer. His prayer provides the key to his life.

From Jabez we learn that *disabilities need not disqualify* in the race of life. That Jabez was born with a tremendous temperamental handicap is implicit in the name given him by his mother, which means "sorrowful." "I bare him with sorrow," she said. Tragedy which struck before his birth shadowed his entry into the world. Prenatal influence can greatly affect the nature of a child and this baby did not escape its influence. Though

his nature was set in a minor key and he inherited
a bias toward pessimism, Jabez soared above his
brothers who inherited no such disability. It may
even be that it was his handicap which made him
great, for disabilities need never disqualify for a
spiritual ministry.

God is sympathetic toward a holy ambition.
Jabez cherished a strong ambition to which God
responded magnificently. His four petitions were
indeed ambitious and on the surface might have
appeared selfish. But the fact that "God granted
him that which he requested" indicates that the
glory of God rather than selfish aggrandizement
was his real desire. God does not honor unworthy
motives, nor does He answer self-centered prayers.
"Ye ask, and receive not, because ye ask amiss, that
ye may consume it upon your lusts" (James 4:3).
God delighted to honor Jabez because Jabez desired to honor God. "Them that honor me, I will
honor" (I Sam. 2:30) is an abiding principle.

The fourfold petition of his prayer voiced the
aspiration of his heart.

He prayed for *Divine enlargement*. "Oh, that
thou wouldest bless me indeed." No ordinary blessing would satisfy him. He yearned for something
which surpassed any previous experience. God's
ear is always attentive to such a plea, for a true
spiritual blessing always ennobles character and
qualifies to bring greater blessing to others. "And
God granted him that which he requested."

He prayed for *Divine enlargement*. "Oh, that
Thou wouldest . . . enlarge my coast." His primary
concern doubtless was for an increase of territory
which would bring him greater influence, but it

was not for mere personal aggrandizement, for
God granted his request. His was a God-sanctioned
ambition. Some of our hymns sound pious but
they do not always stand close analysis. They can
express a dangerous half-truth. Here is one:

> Content to fill a little space,
> If God be glorified.

That is of course, a worthy sentiment. We must
all be willing to glorify God in "a little space" if
that is where He has placed us. Until we qualify
there, it is unlikely that we will be promoted. But
the unintentioned implication of this couplet is
that God can be glorified more in a little space
than in a larger sphere. Should we not be ambitious to fill a larger place if we can thereby bring
more glory to God? God does not want all His
children filling only the small places of life. He
requires those who will serve Him loyally and
glorify Him in great positions of responsibility.
Such contentment as the hymn envisages could
spring from spiritual inertia and unwillingness to
pay the price of occupying larger territory for
Christ.

Would not Carey's motto be more worthy of our
Master? "Attempt great things for God. Expect
great things from God." God is looking for men
who, like Jabez, are discontented with a limited
opportunity when they could bring greater glory
to God in a wider sphere. Our ambition should
be for a wider influence for God, a deeper love
toward God, a stronger faith in God and a growing
knowledge of God. The motive of our ambition
must be carefully watched, but when it is right,

God will not deny our prayer for an enlarged sphere. "And God granted him that which he requested."

His third petition was for *Divine enablement.* "Oh . . . that thine hand might be with me." An enlarged coast involves increased responsibilities and imposes greater demands. Jabez knew he required a power greater than his own to possess and develop this new territory for God. God's hand represents His mighty power. John the Baptist moved Israel so mightily because "the hand of the Lord was with him" (Luke 1:66). So it was with Jabez, for "God granted him that which he requested."

His final request was for *Divine environment.* "Oh . . . that thou wouldst keep me from evil, that it may not grieve me!" Jabez well knew the inevitable peril of an enlarged coast—increased activity on the part of his enemies. Attempting great things for God always attracts the hostile attentions of the Evil One, and Jabez' prayer is appropriate in all ages. "I pray . . . that thou shouldest keep them from the evil one" (John 17:15, A.S.V.) was our Lord's petition for His own. We are very vulnerable to Satan's attacks and need to walk in humble dependence on God. In his conscious need Jabez prayed for a sense of God's environing presence: "And God granted him that which he requested."

There is nothing which God will not do for the man whose sole ambition is for His greater glory.

13

THE WEAPONS OF SPIRITUAL VICTORY

They overcame him.

And there was war in heaven: Michael and his angels fought against the dragon; and the dragon fought and his angels, and prevailed not; neither was their place found any more in heaven. And the great dragon was cast out, that old serpent, called the Devil and Satan, which deceiveth the whole world: he was cast out into the earth, and his angels were cast out with him.

And I heard a loud voice saying in heaven, Now is come salvation, and strength, and the kingdom of our God, and the power of his Christ: for the accuser of our brethren is cast down, which accused them before our God day and night. And they overcame him by the blood of the Lamb, and by the word of their testimony; and they loved not their lives unto the death.—Revelation 12:7-11

IN VIEW OF THE VAST POWER he wields in the world, insufficient attention is paid to the activities and methods of the Devil. We allow him to outwit us in strategy and outmaneuver us in tactics largely because of our ignorance of his devices. Too much goes by default because we are not alive to his insidious activity.

In World War II the victory gained by Field Marshal Montgomery over Rommel was largely due to his painstaking study of his opponent—his character, temperament, habits, and previous tactics. The knowledge gained enabled him so to plot his campaign as to take advantage of the strengths of his own position and weaknesses of his foe.

In the paragraph before us, we are given firsthand information of Satan's character and methods by the One who conquered him, and with it the assurance that we too can overcome.

THE WARFARE

The first eleven chapters of the Book of Revelation unveil the unceasing struggle between the church and the world. The remaining chapters reveal that this outward conflict is but the manifestation of the eternal war between God and Satan, between light and darkness. At the beginning of this section we meet a startling sentence: "And there was war in heaven." This heavenly warfare was very soon manifested on earth for the record continues: "The devil is come down unto you, having great wrath, because he knoweth that he hath but a short time" (v. 12). His anger increases with the shortening of his time, which perhaps explains the mounting tensions of our day.

A survey of church history reveals something of his mode of warfare. When persecution failed to subdue the zeal of the infant church, he incited the Judaizers to debase the Gospel of grace and cause division through their insidious teachings. When this stratagem was defeated and the Gospel finally overthrew paganism in Rome, he brought to birth the Roman and Greek churches with their mixture of truth and error. In our own day, when Africa appeared to be well on the way to complete evangelization, he interposed the Moslem belt across the continent between the advancing church and the unreached heathen.

Every true disciple of Christ is involved in a global war, for our commission is to take the Gospel to the whole creation. We are engaged in total warfare against a ruthless enemy and there are no exemptions from service. The homeland is as much a part of the battle front as the foreign field. It is a war in which there will be casualties.

The Warriors

"They overcame him." In verses 9 and 10 a series of revealing names is given to our enemy. In five vivid words the Holy Spirit gives us searching insight into his character and methods of warfare. He is called *the great dragon.* To the Greek mind the dragon was a fabulous monster, a dread and hostile power, cruel, mysterious, ferocious, malicious.

As *that old serpent* he is cunning and crafty, working under cover. He seldom comes out into the open, but as in Eden hides behind someone else. He even transforms himself into *an angel of light* (II Cor. 11:14).

The designation, *the Devil,* means *slanderer.* In the beginning he slandered God to Adam and Eve, and later he slandered Job to God. Slander is one of his most potent weapons, and he delights when children of God engage in the same ministry of detraction!

Then he is *Satan,* the adversary of God, the Church, and the believer. He is the open enemy of all that is holy. "And he showed me Joshua the high priest standing before the angel of Jehovah [the Lord], and Satan standing at his right hand to be his adversary" (Zech. 3:1, A.S.V.). He is the antagonist of all that is in man's highest interests and to the greater glory of God.

Finally, he is *the accuser of the brethren.* He is the *father of lies* but will tell the truth when it suits his purpose. And we, alas, provide him with so much material to establish his case. Not only does he accuse us to God, but he accuses us to one another. It is striking to note that the word "going" to and fro in the earth, used by Satan to describe his wanderings, suggests "going about as a spy," a commentary on his sinister activities.

If this powerful, malicious, crafty, slanderous, accusing adversary with his highly organized hierarchy is ranged against us, who can overcome him? *"They* overcame him"—the weak, sinful brethren whom he accused to God. As brethren they sustain a blood relationship with their Lord, and this alone makes them the object of satanic hostility. He can now hurt and discredit the Head of the church only through the members of His body. But the same blood relationship enables them to share His victory. If we are to overcome him we must see to our weapons.

THE WEAPONS

Our commander does not ask us to engage in this warfare unarmed. He provides three invincible weapons of offense.

First, there is *the judicial weapon*. "They overcame him by the blood of the Lamb," a weapon which derives its potency from Calvary. The secret of victory is not our prowess, but our union with Christ in His victorious death. The phrase, "the blood of the Lamb," is not to be regarded as a magic charm, something to be imported into sermon or prayer, thus insuring orthodoxy and supernatural results. It is not to be a credulously mumbled formula, not a parroting of mystical words, but the expression of an intelligent, active, vital faith in Christ, the Lamb of God who by the shedding of His blood bruised the serpent's head and finally defeated him.

This is one of the most pregnant phrases in the Scriptures. In it is concentrated all the virtue and value of Christ's mediatorial work. Blood is life in solution. The life of the Lamb of God, violently taken by sinful men, was yet voluntarily laid down. He rose from the dead and ascended to the right hand of God by virtue of His own blood. "The blood of the Lamb" now becomes the ground of our victory. It is to be noted that the "by" in this phrase connotes "because of" not "by means of." Because He broke the power of sin and Satan by the shedding of His blood, we who are united with Him can participate in His victory. We are to regard Satan as already conquered and to claim Christ's victory over him as our own, for Satan has no counter-weapon to "the blood of the Lamb."

So then, when in prayer we plead the blood of the Lamb, we are really saying that our faith is fixed and resting for victory upon all Christ achieved for us by His vicarious death and the victorious resurrection which released unmeasured Divine power. This is our first weapon of offense.

The second weapon in our hands is *the evidential weapon*. "They overcame him . . . by the word of their testimony." Faith in the death of Christ is to be followed by witness to His living, powerful Word. It is not clear whether the reference is to the Word to which they bore testimony or to their testimony itself. Probably both are included. Any testimony which is not Bible-based is powerless to achieve spiritual results, but grounded in the Word it becomes the sword of the Spirit. Note that it is not argument or denunciation but testimony which silences the Devil. The Word of Christ and His apostles, tested in experience, becomes testimony to us. The Word in the intellect is not sufficient in warfare with Satan. Testimony occupied a prominent place in apostolic preaching and Paul used it with great effect. There is room for education, for medicine, for agriculture in the missionary program, but nothing can take the place of the word of our testimony delivered in the power of the Spirit. God has made the world wonderfully accessible to us and has given wings to our testimony in these days. Radio, television, recordings can all be used by Him to overcome the dragon.

Lastly there is *the sacrificial weapon*. "They held their lives cheap and did not shrink even from death" (Weymouth). The Greek word here translated "testimony" is that from which our own word "martyr" is derived. This third weapon, as distinct from the former two, is not directed at our enemy. It is a sword which we take in both hands and plunge into our own breast. Only the sword of testimony of one who has the martyr spirit is mightily effective. To him life is of secondary importance. In this, our Lord has set a shining example to His followers. The sacrifice of His life did not begin at Calvary, or even at Bethlehem. He was "the Lamb slain from the foundation of the world" (Rev. 13:8). He was the exemplification of His own teaching that "except a corn of wheat fall into the ground and die, it abideth alone: but if it die, it bringeth forth much fruit" (John 12:24). The word of our testimony will be sterile unless we too are treading the way of the cross.

Yet there is no single thing so absent from contemporary Christianity as this martyr spirit, this element of sacrifice. Being a Christian today confers blessings rather than costs sacrifice. We are closely wedded to our comforts, as though comfort-loving Christians could be disciples of a cross-bearing Lord!

They overcame him. Here is a note of undefeatable optimism. Our Lord stated categorically: "Upon this rock I will build my church; and the gates of hell shall not prevail against it" (Matt. 16:18). Satan's judgment and defeat were finally secured at Calvary, but until the sentence is executed, we have these invincible weapons. We reckon on the victory of Calvary. We bear testimony to its conquering power. We are willing to lay down life itself for our Commander.

14

THE ART OF PRAYING WITH AUTHORITY

First bind . . . then spoil.

But if I cast out devils by the Spirit of God,
then the kingdom of God is come unto you. Or
else, how can one enter into a strong man's
house, and spoil his goods, except he first bind
the strong man? and then he will spoil his
house. . . . When a strong man armed keepeth
his palace, his goods are in peace: but when a
stronger than he shall come upon him, and
overcome him, he taketh from him all his
armor wherein he trusted, and divideth his
spoils.—Matthew 12:28, 29; Luke 11:21, 22

PRAYER MAY BE RESOLVED into five constituent
elements. Adoration is the soul lost in the won-
dering worship of God. Thanksgiving is the heart
overflowing in grateful appreciation of His many
mercies. Confession is the expression in words of
genuine contrition, of a sense of sin and failure
to attain to the Divine standard. Petition is the
laying of personal needs before a loving heavenly
Father. Intercession is request for others who do
not stand in the same place of privilege and who

do not enjoy the same access into the presence of God. Each of these elements of prayer will find its place in a well-balanced devotional life.

Within the ministry of intercession there may be contrasting spiritual activity. Our intercession may be the calm expression of a restful faith: "Ask, and it shall be given you" (Matt. 7:7). "He that cometh to God must believe that he is, and that he is a rewarder of them that diligently seek him" (Heb. 11:6). Or it may be expressed in spiritual conflict: "I would that ye knew what great conflict I have for you" (Col. 2:1). "Epaphras . . . saluteth you, always laboring fervently for you in prayers" (Col. 4:12). "We wrestle . . . against principalities, against powers" (Eph. 6:12). This latter aspect of prayer is too little known and practiced, but the mastery of what has been called "prayer warfare" will change defeat into victory in many a situation.

In the passages which head this chapter, Christ was trenchantly refuting the ridiculous charge of the Pharisees that He was exorcising demons by the power of the prince of demons. As though the Devil would be naïve enough to destroy his own kingdom! Jesus pointed out that surely His casting out demons indicated His mastery over their prince rather than subservience to him.

"THE STRONG MAN"

This graphic pictorial representation of authoritative praying presents us with "a strong man armed," who keeps his palace and his goods in peace until "a stronger than he" overcomes him and divides the spoil. "The strong man" is the

Devil whose power over the souls and minds of men is mighty though limited. The "stronger than he" is none other than the Lamb because of whose blood we can overcome the powers of darkness (Rev. 12:11).

The Lamb is engaged in deathless conflict with "the strong man," and He will not rest until he is overcome and his palace utterly despoiled. And in this conflict between rival kingdoms the intercessor fills an important role. But he will never play his part with the fullest effectiveness unless he has a vivid sense of the victory of Christ gained over the Devil at the cross. He must constantly recognize and count on the fact that Satan is a vanquished foe since Calvary.

It was the discovery of this aggressive aspect of prayer which turned defeat into victory in the experience of the apostle to the Lisu people of Southwest China, Mr. James O. Fraser. He had worked for five years with great devotion and self-sacrifice, but with little to show for it. Not only was he discouraged in his work, but he had almost reached the point of desperation in his own inner experience. Deliverance and blessing came through reading an article in a magazine which had been sent to him. Here is his own account:

> What it showed me was that deliverance from the power of the evil one comes through definite resistance on the ground of the cross. I had found that much of the spiritual teaching one hears does not seem to work. My apprehension at any rate of other aspects of truth had broken down. The passive side of leaving everything to the Lord Jesus as our life, while

blessedly true, was not all that was needed just then. . . . We need different truth at different times. Definite resistance on the ground of the cross was what brought me light, for I found that it worked. I found that I *could* have victory in the spiritual realm whenever I wanted it. . . . One had to learn gradually how to use this new-found weapon of resistance.

Being an engineer by profession, Mr. Fraser was always interested in seeing things work, and as he began to apply this truth so new to him, he was thrilled to find he had not been misled. Not only did new victory come into his life, but the longed-for blessing was poured out upon his beloved Lisu, a trickle which grew into a mighty stream.

"First Bind . . . Then . . . Spoil"

It is by no means impossible that our failure to recognize the priorities indicated in Scripture is a potent cause of lack of effectiveness in our witness. Christ said we must first bind "the strong man" before we can spoil his goods. "No one can go into a strong man's house and carry off his property, unless he first binds the strong man, and then he will plunder his house" (Mark 3:27, Weymouth). Are we at pains to observe this order so clearly enunciated by our Lord, or do we unsuccessfully try to plunder his house while he is still unfettered? If so, it is little wonder that in so many cases he has snatched back souls we have endeavored to deliver from his clutches. It is this heartbreaking experience which has discouraged so many missionaries, who have seen people make profession of faith and then have watched them sucked back into the vortex of heathenism. Too much of our praying is merely the repeated offering of an earnest petition rather than what Jesus referred to as binding "the strong man."

So that we may understand what is meant by this expression we will consider the way in which our Lord Himself bound him. He had three great encounters with the Devil—in the wilderness, in the garden, and on Golgotha. In the wilderness He achieved His first victory by successfully resisting the temptation which assailed Him along the only three avenues by which it can reach man— appetite, avarice, and ambition. Each phase of temptation He rebutted with the Sword of the Spirit, and the Devil, vanquished, left Him for a season. Because of this triumph Jesus was able to confidentially claim: "The prince of this world cometh, and hath nothing in me" (John 14:30). We shall be powerless to effect the practical binding of Satan if there are unyielded areas in our lives which give him a hold over us.

Our Lord's next major encounter with the Devil was in the Garden of Gethsemane. So intense and agonizing was His conflict that, contrary to nature, the blood forced its way through His pores. And how did He triumph on this occasion? By merging His will in the will of His Father. There is a striking progression in His prayers.

"He . . . kneeled down, and prayed, saying, Father, if thou be willing, remove this cup from me: nevertheless not my will, but thine, be done" (Luke 22:41, 42).

"He went away again the second time, and

prayed, saying O my Father, if this cup may not pass away from me, except I drink it, thy will be done" (Matt. 26:42).

In the second prayer, the reluctance of the human will evidenced in the first petition has been lost in glad acceptance of the Divine will. There is no "My will and Thy will" but only "Thy will." He is now able to cry, not with mere acceptance, but with exultation: "The cup which my Father hath given me, shall I not drink it?" (John 18:11).

Thus Satan suffered another shattering defeat as the Lord steadfastly refused to move from complete and joyous acceptance of His Father's will even though it involved death on the cross. With us too there must be an unquestioning acceptance of the will of God if we are to remain in the place of victory.

The complete and final defeat of the Devil was consummated at Golgotha, where Christ triumphed over him in His death. "And the hostile princes and rulers He shook off from Himself, and boldly displayed them as His conquests, when by the Cross He triumphed over them" (Col. 2:15, Weymouth). Was not the very purpose of His Incarnation "that through death he might destroy him that had the power of death . . . the devil"? (Heb. 2:14).

The word "destroy" used in the latter passage means "to render inoperative, to put out of action" and the same idea is involved in the command to "bind" the strong man. By His death our Lord forever broke the power of the Devil over the believer. Henceforth he was a usurper. Any dominion he now exercises over us is either because we fail to apprehend and appropriate the completeness of Christ's triumph, or is the result of sin tolerated in our lives, which provides a vantage ground for his activities. Let us firmly grasp the fact that Christ has "destroyed" and "bound" the Devil, and as members of His Body, united to Him by a living faith, sharing the same life, we may participate in His victory. The victory was our Lord's victory. The final execution of the sentence on Satan will be by Him to whom all judgment has been committed. But He identifies us with Him in this victory. His triumph becomes ours.

POTENTIAL AND ACTUAL

The practical question arises: How does this victory over Satan become actual and operative in the sphere which is our special concern? It is not sufficient to know that on the cross Christ potentially delivered every soul from Satan's power. The potential must be translated into the actual and this is done when we exercise the spiritual authority which has been given to us.

When the Seventy returned radiant from their journey of witness, rejoicing that even the demons were subject to them, Jesus made an amazing statement, the full significance of which is seldom realized. "And he said unto them, I beheld Satan fallen as lightning from heaven. Behold, I have given you authority . . . over all the power of the enemy . . ." (Luke 10:18, 19, A.S.V.). We are in no less privileged position than were these early disciples.

In this utterance Jesus linked with the overthrow of Satan, the delegation to His disciples of authority over *all* the power of the enemy, an authority which they could use in any situation and at any time. As they wielded this authority, they found that it worked and even demons were subject to them. "In my name" (that is, by His authority) "shall ye cast out demons" (Mark 16:17, A.S.V.). Similarly, by making use of Christ's authority, we may bind Satan and then confidently "spoil his house."

But in doing this we must be sure of our ground. Acts 19 records the attempt of the seven sons of Sceva "vagabond Jews, exorcists," to exercise authority over Satan and evil spirits. When their own attempts at exorcism failed, they tried to use an authority they did not possess. "We adjure you by Jesus whom Paul preacheth," they commanded. But recognizing the fraud, the demon in the possessed man replied: "Jesus I know, and Paul I know: but who are ye?" (Acts 19:15). "And the man in whom the evil spirit was leaped on them, and overcame them . . . so that they fled out of the house naked and wounded" (Acts 19:16). It is a solemn thing to pretend to an authority which has not been conferred. The powers of darkness are not to be treated lightly.

Jesus was well known to the demons, and feared by them, too. "I know thee who thou art, the Holy One of God" (Mark 1:24), was the unbidden testimony. "Art thou come hither to torment us before the time?" (Matt. 8:29). For thirty years they had watched Jesus' sinless life and knew they had no hold over Him. They were acquainted with Paul too. Had they not rejoiced in his thirst for

Christian blood? And had they not been dismayed at his complete transformation on the Damascus Road which made him their most dreaded foe? Yes, they were acquainted with Paul. But they did not know these vagabond Jews. Their names were not known in Hell. Are our names known to the powers of darkness or are we spiritual nonentities, offering no threat to their kingdom? Are our prayers effectual in binding "the strong man" or does he laugh at our puny attempts to spoil his house?

NEEDLESS IMPOTENCE

The father of the demon-possessed boy lamented over the very disciples on whom Christ had bestowed His authority over all the power of the enemy when he said "they could not" exorcise the demon. When they asked the Lord: "Why could not we cast him out?" He diagnosed the cause in one word—unbelief (Matt. 17:20, 21). They had no vital faith in the authority He had given them and their unbelief had paralyzed them. When we find ourselves involved in a situation for which our human power is totally inadequate, it is for us, making use of Christ's authority, to claim the victory He won on the cross and to maintain the stand of faith until the victory becomes manifest. Is this not what the apostle meant by fighting the fight of faith?

God taught this lesson to James O. Fraser as, with a deepening conviction begotten by the Holy Spirit, he claimed in prayer more than one hundred Lisu families. He wrote:

Satan's tactics seem to be as follows, he will first of all oppose our breaking through to the place of faith, for it is an authoritative "notice to quit." He does not so much mind carnal, rambling prayers, for they do not hurt him much. That is why it is so difficult to attain to a definite faith in God for a definite object. We often have to strive and wrestle in prayer (Eph. 6:10) before we attain this quiet restful faith. And until we break right through and *join hands with God,* we have not attained to real faith at all. . . . However, once we attain to a *real faith,* all the forces of hell are impotent to annul it. . . . The real battle begins when the prayer of faith is offered.

Making use of Christ's authority and participating in His victory we can be instrumental in binding "the strong man" in any given spiritual situation. Only then will we be in a position to spoil his goods and deliver his captives.

15

SPIRITUAL FERVOR, FALSE
AND TRUE

Concerning zeal . . . —Philippians 3:6
The zeal of thine house hath eaten me up.
—John 2:17

ZEAL OF THE RIGHT SORT is a quality to be coveted. The meaning of the word according to Webster is "ardor in the pursuit of anything; ardent and active interest; enthusiasm; fervor." Unfortunately this word which connotes such desirable characteristics has become debased in meaning and is often attributed to one who is very enthusiastic but rather lacking in balance and intelligence.

Although zeal is not a distinctively Christian word, it has a definite place in the Christian vocabulary. It can be manifested in any of life's activities, whether secular or sacred. All who have achieved great things in the service of God or man have been characterized by a consuming zeal which enabled them to overleap all obstacles in the pursuit of their goal.

Our Lord displayed this quality to a unique degree from earliest years. It was zeal for His Father's house and interests which drew the undeserved rebuke from His parents when He was only twelve years old. Throughout the whole of His earthly life His ardor persisted unabated until it led Him to the cross.

FALSE ZEAL

Much that passes for spiritual zeal it only fleshly energy. It is "soulish" rather than spiritual. Nor is religious zeal confined to evangelical believers. Did ever cult display such feverish zeal as Jehovah's Witnesses? The Al Azhar University in Cairo is reported to be training and sending out 5,000 Moslem missionaries every year to conquer the world for Mohammed. On May 13, 1957, 2,500 young men were admitted into the Buddhist priesthood in Thailand—commemorating the 2,500th year of Buddha. Mankind has never witnessed a more fanatical zeal than that manifested by communists around the globe in their passion for world revolution.

Paul did not lack zeal before his conversion, but it was tragically misdirected. I "was zealous toward God," he affirmed in his defense (Acts 22:3). But his zeal led him into grievous excesses. When recounting his supposed advantages as a faithful Jew, he included: "Concerning zeal, persecuting the church" (Phil. 3:6), for "being exceedingly mad against them, I persecuted them even unto strange cities" (Acts 26:11). After his experience on the road to Damascus, his mistaken zeal became one of his greatest griefs. "I am the least of the apostles, that I am not meet to be called an apostle," he mourned, "because I persecuted the church of God" (I Cor. 15:9). He could never forgive himself, but he reveled in the forgiving love of

God "who . . . counted me faithful, putting me into the ministry: who was before a blasphemer, and a persecutor, and injurious; but I obtained mercy, because I did it ignorantly in unbelief" (I Tim. 1:12, 13). Misdirected zeal can work havoc with the church of God.

MISUNDERSTOOD ZEAL

Because He was so conspicuously different from all other men, His foes described Jesus as a demoniac. "The people answered and said, Thou hast a devil" (John 7:20). His friends placed a more kindly construction on His unusual actions and explained that He was not responsible for them. "When his friends heard of it, they went out to lay hold on him: for they said, He is beside himself" (Mark 3:21). How amazing that the only perfectly balanced Man in the world should be so regarded by His contemporaries!

The word "zeal" is derived from the Greek verb "to boil," and signifies an ardor, an enthusiasm which irresistibly boils up in the heart. When His disciples saw their Master ablaze with holy zeal and flaming with sinless anger, disturbing the rhythm of centuries by driving traders and moneychangers from the temple, they suddenly realized the significance of the prophecy in Psalm 69:9. "His disciples remembered that it was written, The zeal of thine house hath eaten me up" (John 2:17).

"It is enough for the disciple that he be as his master, and the servant as his lord," Jesus warned. "If they have called the master of the house Beelzebub, how much more shall they call them of his household?" (Matt. 10:25). It was not strange therefore that Paul should share the misunderstanding of His Lord. "Festus said with a loud voice, Paul, thou art beside thyself; much learning doth make thee mad" (Acts 26:24).

And yet is it not strange that the apostle of Christian sanity should be considered mentally unbalanced? It is true that compared with others of his day Paul's activities were hardly normal, but sanity is a relative term. It depends on who does the judging. It was not standard practice to act as Paul did in Ephesus, when he challenged the believers: "Remember that by the space of three years I ceased not to warn every one night and day with tears" (Acts 20:31), but was this not the evidence of truest sanity? Paul had both this world and the next in correct perspective and acted accordingly.

Lord, give me this very day a burning zeal
For souls immortal; enable me to plead with such
With earnestness intense, love strong as death,
And faith God-given. Will the world cry—"Mad"?
I would be mad; such madness be my joy,
For thrice it blesses: first my own cold heart,
Then glorifies my God, and plucks perchance
My sin-stained brother from the jaws of death.

—ANONYMOUS

In Romans 12:11 Paul exhorts the believers not to slacken in their zeal, but in the same chapter he encourages them to cultivate Christian sanity. So in his thinking, zeal and sanity were not necessarily mutually exclusive. E. M. Blaiklock translates Romans 12:3: "For as God in His grace has enabled me, I charge everyone of you not to think more highly of himself than he ought to think but to cultivate Christian sanity, according as God has given to every man faith as a measure." Paul is deprecating self-esteem and inculcating sane thinking. The word he uses, *sophrusune,* combines the ideas of moderation and self-control, that delicate balance of mind which does not fly to extremes. And yet this is the man who is accused of being beside himself because of his excess zeal for his Master.

TRUE ZEAL

A. W. Tozer thus contrasts true and false zeal:

The pure love of God and men which expresses itself in a burning desire to advance God's glory, and leads to poured-out devotion to the temporal and eternal welfare of our fellowmen is certainly approved of God; but the nervous squirrel-cage activity of self-centered and ambitious religious leaders is just as certainly offensive to Him, and will prove at last to have been injurious to the souls of countless millions of human beings.

True zeal has Christ as its object and inspiration. Count Zinzendorf claimed: "I have only one passion; it is He, He alone." And his Christ-centered zeal sparked into being one of the world's greatest missionary organizations, the Moravian Church.

Frederic W. H. Myers explains Paul's flaming zeal in glowing words:

Christ, I am Christ's, and let that name suffice you,
    Ay, for me too He greatly hath sufficed;

Lo, with no winning words I would entice you,
   Paul has no honor and no friend but Christ.

.   .   .   .

Yes, through life, death, through sorrow and through
      sinning
He shall suffice me, for He hath sufficed;
Christ is the end, for Christ is the beginning,
   Chirst the beginning, for the end is Christ.

Christ-centered zeal will have varying manifesta-
tions. It impelled Paul to seek lost men for Christ,
"night and day, with tears." It drove Epaphras to
intense prayer for his fellow Christians in Colosse:
"Epaphras . . . a servant of Christ, saluteth you,
always laboring fervently for you in prayers. . . .
For I bear him record, that he hath a great zeal for
you" (Col. 4:12, 13). It produced in the Mace-
donian colonists provocative liberality. "As touch-
ing the ministering to the saints . . . your zeal hath
provoked very many" (II Cor. 9:1, 2). Even the
death of Christ had as one of its objectives the
creating of "a peculiar people, zealous of good
works" (Titus 2:14). True zeal always bears a
spiritual harvest.

Paul's ideal for his converts, as reflected in his
prayers, was a mind aflame with the truth of God,
a heart burning with love for God and man, and a
will ablaze with a passion for God's glory. It is
true that we evangelicals need more scholarship,
but even more do we need incandescent zeal for
Christ. The combination of deep knowledge and
flaming zeal may be rare but they are not incompatible. The brilliant Henry Martyn cried as he
stood for the first time on Indian soil, "Now let
me burn out for God." Within seven short years

his zeal had literally consumed him. But before he died he had translated the New Testament into three languages! His statement inspired these words:

And when I am dying, how glad I shall be
That the lamp of my life has been blazed out for
    Thee.
  I shall not care in whatever I gave
  Of labor or money one sinner to save.
I shall not care that the way has been rough
That Thy dear feet led the way is enough.
  And when I am dying, how glad I shall be
  That the lamp of my life has been blazed out for
    Thee.

FLAGGING ZEAL

Paul's knowledge that zeal always tends to evaporate inspired his exhortations to diligence. Few of us maintain the zeal of early youth. We begin so well but fail to carry through. It would seem that Paul noticed this tendency in young Timothy. Fearing lest he become a spent force, he counseled him: "Stir up the gift of God, which is in thee" (II Tim. 1:6).

In the Solomon Islands the natives sleep around a fire which is their only blanket. The nights are chilly, and as the body temperature gradually drops, they huddle closer around the blaze. From time to time one and another rises to place fresh fuel on the dying fire, so that they may enjoy its warmth. The church at Ephesus was in similar condition. The flame of their early love for Christ had waned to a few feeble embers and their Lord counseled them to rise and place fresh fuel on the fire of their devotion, lest their lamp of witness be removed.

Tepid Christians have no awakening ministry, nor do they atract others to Christ. It is the zealous man who impresses his generation, whose preaching leaves saving impressions on the minds of men. To John the Baptist Jesus bore this wonderful testimony: "He was a burning and shining light" (John 5:35). And light always shines at the expense of the wick. Adolph Deissmann explained the unabating zeal of Paul in these words: "The lighting of Damascus found plenty of inflammable material in the soul of the young persecutor. We see the flames shoot up, and we feel that the glow then kindled lost none of its glow in Paul the aged."

MAINTAINED ZEAL

Instead of "fervent in spirit" in the central phrase of Romans 12:11, Dr. H. C. Lees gives this felicitous paraphrase, "Kept at boiling point by the Spirit." Between our diligence in the service of man (v. 11a) and our bond service for the Master (v. 11c) is this central furnace to keep our spirits "fairly seething with enthusiasm." It is comparatively easy to reach boiling point at some moment of spiritual exaltation, but it is not so easy to stay there. We can neither generate nor maintain our own zeal. If it is not to "flag" there must be some external stimulus and this is provided by the fire of the Holy Spirit. And the power generated must not evaporate in unutilized steam, but be harnessed to do bond service for the Master. It is of supreme importance then, that we maintain a correct relationship to the Holy Spirit, and that we do not grieve Him. Christian, in *Pilgrim's Progress,* saw the flame of fire on the hearth in the Interpreter's house, and one sprinkling it with water, yet the flame rose higher and higher. He marveled at this phenomenon until he saw One behind pouring on oil. It is the work of the Spirit constantly to pour oil on the fire and to keep our zeal at boiling point. Apollos was a glowing example of His ministry. Apollos . . . "being fervent in spirit, he spake and taught diligently the things of the Lord" (Acts 18:25).

Fifty days after the resurrection, the facts of the Gospel were complete and common knowledge, but nothing significant happened until the Holy Spirit descended. But after His advent, the Christians were so filled with holy zeal and passion that the Jews could explain it only as drunkenness, confusing the Devil's stimulant with the Divine Stimulus.

It is possible for us to be "kept at boiling point by the Spirit." "Thinking enough, meditating enough, musing enough on Christ will do it," wrote Alexander Whyte. "Yes, if you will, you can think, and read, and pray yourself into the possession of a heart as hot as Paul's heart. For the same Holy Spirit as gave Christ His hot heart and Paul his hot heart is given to you also."

16

THE WAY OF UNQUESTIONING DISCIPLESHIP

What is that to thee? Follow thou me.—John 21:23

TESTED SAINTS in all ages have been prone to complain with Israel, "the way of the Lord is not equal" (Ezek. 18:29). Some of God's dealings seem to contradict our innate sense of fairness, some of our fellows appear to receive preferential treatment, and instead of faithfully discharging our responsibilities, we are tempted to look over our shoulder at others.

This was a tendency of Peter the apostle with which our Lord dealt very faithfully on two occasions. At times there seemed to be a touch of ruthlessness or at least of acerbity in the Lord's response to what appeared to be harmless inquiries, and the fisherman received more than his share of rebuffs at the hand of Him who was meekness and love incarnate. Surely Peter's well-intentioned suggestion that the Master might be a little easier on Himself hardly merited the terrible rebuke: "Get thee behind me, Satan; thou art an offense unto me" (Matt. 16:23). And did not his innocuous inquiry about John's future, "What shall this man do?" (John 21:21), meet with too harsh a reception in the words: "What is that to thee? Follow thou me"—a polite way of saying, "Mind your own business, Peter"? Was not our Lord's warning that "many that are first shall be last; and the last shall be first," a rather chilling response to Peter's reasonable question: "Lo, we have left all, and followed thee"? Did the Lord take delight in baiting Peter, or was He seeking to underscore an important truth? There was undoubtedly an underlying reason for the sternness of our Lord's words which has relevance for all His servants today.

Jesus had just concluded His tender yet soul-searching interview with the now humbled and penitent Peter. In response to the Master's thrice-repeated question, he had made his renewed protestation of love and had received a fresh commission. Then had followed the prophetic intimation of the violent death by which he would glorify God, and the final injunction, "Follow me" (John 21:15-19).

AN IRRELEVANT QUESTION

One would have thought that the moving experiences of the past few hours would have sufficed to concentrate Peter's attention on the Master who had so graciously restored and recommissioned him. But no! Instead of being occupied with the Lord, he gets busy comparing his own future with that of John. Immediately his mind flies off on a tangent, and with ever-ready tongue he blurts out, "Lord, and what shall this man do?" In His customary manner Jesus answers Peter's captious question with another: "If I will that he tarry till I come, what is that to thee? Follow thou me."

Peter was intruding into a realm which was no concern of his. In the shock of learning that he would have to tread the pathway of rejection and suffering, his first reaction was to compare his lot with that of others. Is he being discriminated against? Will John be exempt from the hardships he must endure? Will John be bound and carried whither he would not, or will he be accorded preferential treatment? It is not difficult to sense the beginnings of a new self-pity. Instead of answering his elliptical question, Jesus sharply rebuked Peter's curiosity. "What is that to thee? Follow thou me." He who had just asserted His right to determine and reveal Peter's future, now asserts His rights over John: "If I will that he tarry till I come. . . ."

The fact is that Peter was being trained in the school of Christ for supremely important work in the interests of the kingdom, and he must learn his lessons thoroughly. In his following of Jesus he must never turn about and compare his lot with that of another disciple. His constant temptation was to try to manage other people's affairs. Did he not on one occasion even try to manage Jesus? He must learn that his Master deals with each of His disciples individually and in ways which are not always clear or explicable to others. No disciple has any business to concern himself with the way the Lord is dealing with another, or to compare his lot with theirs. Did Peter but know it, John would drink of the cup of suffering as deeply as he, but that was no concern of his. His sole care was to follow his Lord, watching his own walk, and discharging his responsibility to feed the flock of God (vv. 15-17).

SELF-PITY OR SELF-SCRUTINY

It is noteworthy that Jesus offered no explanation or interpretation of His rebuke, for no obligation rests on the sovereign Lord to explain Himself to His disciple. He simply made it crystal clear that Peter was meddling in a matter which was no concern of his. He offered no word of comfort, for to administer comfort now would be to indulge weakness and induce self-pity. Peter was a soldier about to engage in relentless warfare, and he must have rigorous training. Here then is the background of these words of stern rebuke. Jesus wants heroes, not busybodies. He must have those who without self-pity render unquestioning obedience to His command. He gives no quarter even to natural and temperamental weakness. He allows Peter to smart under the rebuke. He does not even correct his mistaken assumption that John would not die. He just said in effect, "Suppose it were My good pleasure that he tarry till I come, what business is it of yours? Your concern should be to keep on following Me, and not fretting over whether your brother-disciple is going to receive preferential treatment."

Earlier Peter had shown the same tendency. The rich young ruler, possessed by his possessions, had turned away sorrowful. Pointing the moral, Jesus remarked with what difficulty a rich man entered the kingdom of God. The ever-ready Peter with conscious superiority over the young ruler inter-

posed with: "Behold, we have forsaken all, and
followed thee: what shall we have therefore?"
(Matt. 19:27). Peter doubtless expected that superior devotion would gain precedence at the last
day. And he was right. The Lord assured him
that those who had sacrificially followed Him
would receive an hundredfold here and inherit
eternal life there. But He added a solemn rider:
"Many that are first shall be last; and the last shall
be first" (v. 30). Peter must not compare himself
favorably with the young ruler, but must scrutinize
the motive of his own service.

Motive and Recompense

The motive behind the renunciation was all-important. Peter said: "We have forsaken all . . .
what shall we have?" Jesus indicated that the motive which received the hundredfold recompense
was "for my name's sake" (v. 29). When the para-
mount motive of service is that we may get something, we miss that for which we aim. When our
motive is love for Christ, He is careful to see that
we are not losers—"an hundredfold . . . everlasting life." The first are last, and the last first.

The same principle is apparent in the subsequent parable of the householder who hired laborers to work in his vineyard (Matt. 20:1-16).
When those who had been engaged at daybreak
saw that the latecomers, who had been engaged at
the eleventh hour, received the same remuneration
as they themselves, they began to feel sore. True,
they had received the wage agreed upon—and a
fair wage too—but were they being treated fairly?
When they voiced their complaint, the householder

met them with two unanswerable propositions. First, "Friend, I do thee no wrong." He had fulfilled his just contract with them. He had not defrauded them. From the standpoint of justice they had no case. Second, "Have I not a right to do what I choose with my own property? Or are you envious because I am generous?" (Matt. 20:15, 16, Weymouth). His generosity hurt no one but himself.

The reward was not according to the length of time worked but according to the faithful use of the opportunity granted. The trouble with the twelve-hour laborers is clear from their two unwarranted complaints: "They supposed that they should have received more," and "thou hast made them equal unto us."

Thus the sovereign Lord made clear to Peter that He would not be dictated to concerning His dealings with His other disciples—it remains His sole prerogative. He wrongs no one if He appears to be more generous or lenient with one than with another. He can do what He wills with His own.

The personal application is clear. If the Lord appears to treat others with more generosity, bestowing on them what He withholds from us, if He permits the dark clouds of sorrow and suffering to shadow our hearts while they apparently bask in constant sunshine, how are we to react? First, we should remember that as yet we see through a glass, darkly. We know only in part. Things may be more equal than appears on the surface. Who knows the hidden grief and burden of another's heart?

SECRET BALLAST

When at the height of his well-deserved fame, David Livingstone, the great missionary-explorer, said to an admiring well-wisher: "There is a kindly hand which behind the scenes applies the ballast, when to all outward appearance we are sailing gloriously with the wind." His secret ballast was an erring son who was causing him great sorrow.

We should accept it as axiomatic that God's dealings with our fellow-disciples are no concern of ours. "If I will . . . what is that to thee?" Our business is to watch our motives carefully, to keep our eyes on the Lord whom we follow, and not to look over our shoulders at others.

This principle is not without special relevance on the mission field as well as in the homeland, for the sins of covetousness and envy can thrive in either place, not to mention the sin of murmuring. Do others receive larger personal gifts, more lavish outfit and equipment? Do others appear to receive preferential treatment? Do we envy the greater natural gifts or more attractive personality of others? Do others seem less conscientious in the use of time or money, or in conduct of their work? Has someone received promotion which we felt was our due? Are we misunderstood and our work unappreciated? Do we experience more hardship or enjoy less comforts and conveniences than others in the same circle? Do others enjoy success which is denied to us?

The Lord answers our problem in the simple challenging word: "What is that to thee? Follow thou me." It is not for us to fret over our Lord's dealing with another. We can rest assured that he is being disciplined by the same loving Hand, although it may be in another direction. We can learn the blessedness which comes from finding no cause of stumbling in the Lord or in His disciplining of ourselves or others. We should cheerfully recognize and rejoice in the fact that others may do what we cannot and enjoy what we have not. Our dealings must be directly with God. Our whole concern should be to see that whatever others may do, we like Caleb may "wholly follow the Lord."

17

THE STRATEGIC USE OF TIME

Redeeming the time.—Ephesians 5:16

BUSY CHRISTIAN WORKERS are apt to borrow from the world the expression heard so often: "I don't have the time," or "I am too busy." While it is usually uttered in great sincerity, it is frequently untrue, but the inner attitude it betrays can play havoc with the nervous system and consequently with the spiritual life as well. Is it really true that we do not have enough time? Great men and women never give the impression of being too busy but rather appear to be quite at leisure. It is usually the small and inefficient person who gives the impression of great busyness.

In one of the world's great sermons, "Every Man's Life a Plan of God," by Horace Bushnell, an illuminating paragraph occurs:

> Every human soul has a complete and perfect plan cherished for it in the heart of God, a Divine biography which it enters into life to live. This life, rightly unfolded, will be a complete and beautiful whole, led on by God and unfolded by His secret nurture, as the trees and the flowers by the secret nurture of the world.

159

This statement enshrines a wonderful and transforming truth which, rightly apprehended, could impart a dignity and significance to the humblest life. It accords with Paul's claim that "we are his workmanship, created in Christ Jesus unto good works, which God hath before ordained that we should walk in them" (Eph. 2:10). If this is true, the corollary is that there are enough hours in each day for us to fulfill God's perfect and particular plan for our lives.

CHRIST'S EXAMPLE

Our Lord moved through life with majestic and measured tread, never in a hurry and yet always thronged by demanding crowds, never giving those who sought His help a sense that He had any more important concerns than their particular interests. What was His secret? Knowing that every man's life is a plan of God, He realized that His life and all the conditions in which it was to be worked out were alike under the perfect control of His Father. Time held no power over Him. On several occasions He asserted that His hour had not yet come, and implicit in this assertion was the consciousness that His Father's plan had been drawn with such meticulous accuracy that every hour was accounted for and adjusted to the over-all purpose of His life. His calendar had been arranged, and His sole concern on earth was to fulfill the work given Him to do in the allotted hours (John 7:6; 12:23, 27; 13:1; 17:1). Nor would He allow His much-loved mother to interfere with this Divinely planned timetable (John 2:4). Deep human affection could not be permitted to anticipate His schedules by two days, or His Father's plan would be marred (John 11:6, 9). Small wonder then, that at the close of life He could review it with absolute complacency and utter the self-approving words: "I have finished the work which thou gavest me to do" (John 17:4), no part of it having been marred by undue haste or imperfectly completed through lack of time. He found sufficient time in the twenty-four hours of the day to do the whole will of God. The Lord's corrective word to His disciples: "Are there not twelve hours in the day?" seems to suggest a quiet, steady confidence in His Father's purpose and the resulting courage even in face of confronting enemies and danger. Interruptions could not disturb His peace because they had already been provided for in the Father's planning, and the wrath of enemies would have to await His "hour." Thus He could pursue His work unmoved, knowing it would be "finished." There would be time for all that God meant Him to do, though there might not always be "leisure so much as to eat."

It is easy to stand afar off and admire in our Lord these desirable qualities which so often are lacking in our own lives. But He is to be followed, not only admired, for He left us an example in this as in all else. We have the same Holy Spirit who indwelt Him to help us. Was Christ sent to earth to fulfill His Father's plan? Was it not said anticipatively of Him: "Lo, I come: in the volume of the book it is written of me. I delight to do thy will, O my God" (Ps. 40:7, 8)? Then He says to us: "As the Father hath sent me, even so send I you," and He who sends will enable to fulfill our ministry.

WHAT IS TIME?

Is time the ticking of the clock, the moving of a shadow? Calendar and clock are only mechanical means by which we record our consciousness of time, not time itself. As we commonly use the word it means "duration," or "a stretch of duration in which things happen." But perhaps the most helpful definition of time is "duration turned to account." Dr. John R. Mott viewed time as our lives measured out to us for work, the measure of the capacity of our lives.

Paul counseled the Ephesian believers to "redeem the time," or as Weymouth renders it, "buy up the opportunities," for time is opportunity. Note that time becomes ours by purchase—it has to be redeemed, bought. We exchange it for certain occupations and activities, important or otherwise, and herein lies the importance of a planned life. When we say we don't have time, it may only be that we do not know how to make use of the opportunity time affords us. Time is a God-given stewardship for which we must render account and our use of it will determine the value of our contribution to our day and generation. The difference between one man and another lies largely in his use of time. "All attainments and achievements are conditioned by the full use of time," wrote a master of that art. "If we progress in the economy of time, we are learning to live. If we fail here, we fail everywhere. No man is or does more than his time allows him to do." In his *Holy*

Living Jeremy Taylor wrote: "God hath given to man a short time here upon earth and yet upon this short time eternity depends. No man is a better merchant than he that lays out his time upon God."

The solemn thing about time is, of course, that it can be lost and time lost can never be regained. It cannot be hoarded; it must be spent. It cannot be postponed; it is irretrievably lost. How supremely important, then, that we make full use of the time allotted to us for the fulfillment of our life purpose! The following quotation engraved on a sundial underlines this truth:

> The shadow by my finger cast
> Divides the future from the past;
>   Before it stands the unborn hour
>   In darkness and beyond thy power.
> Behind its unreturning line
> The vanished hour, no longer thine,
>   One hour alone is in thine hands,
>   The NOW on which the shadow stands.

But it is this very fact, this solemn responsibility, which weighs so heavily upon the sensitive conscience when achievement does not match opportunity and produces a sense of guilt. An atmosphere of rush invades the whole of life, not excluding the devotional, and tends to incapacitate for spiritual ministry. There is so much to be done that the hours of the day are increased by reducing sleep. But this can be a highly dangerous expedient if pressed too far. The truth is that if we do not have sufficient time to discharge our responsibilities, we either have undertaken responsibilities not laid upon us by the Lord, or we are not making strategic use of the time He has given us.

We can check on ourselves by keeping a strict
analysis of our lives for one week and this would
be a valuable experiment for each to make. Begin
this very day and put the clock on yourself from
the time you rise until you retire. You will make
some startling revelations and will discover that
you have much more time than you are productive-
ly using. Before saying that we do not have time
for certain activities we should first satisfy ourselves that we are making effective use of the hours
we have.

Each week has 168 hours. Let us allow a generous 56 hours for sleep and rest; 21 hours for meals
and family devotions; 56 hours for work and study.
There still remain 35 hours, or 5 hours a day.
What happens to them? How are they invested?
These are the crucial hours of life which determine
whether our lives will be commonplace or extraordinary. These are the hours which we so frequently allow to slip from us. Our spare time—
and it is not true to say we have no spare time—
is at once our danger and our opportunity.

MASTERY OF TIME

"I think one of the cant phrases of our day is the
familiar one by which we express our permanent
want of time. We repeat it so often that by the
very repetition we have deceived ourselves into
believing it. It is never the supremely busy men
who have no time. So compact and systematic is
the regulation of their day that, whenever you
make a demand upon them, they seem to find additional corners to offer for unselfish service. I con-
fess, as a minister, that the men to whom I most

hopefully look for additional service are the busiest men." So wrote Dr. J. H. Jowett.

Let us face the fact squarely and without equivocation. Each of us has as much time as anyone else in the world. Others may have more money, ability, influence, but we each have twenty-four hours in a day. As in the parable of the pounds, we are each entrusted with the same amount of time, but not all so use it as to produce a tenfold return. True, we do not all have the same capacity, but that fact is recognized in the parable, and the reward for the servant with smaller capacity, but who was equally faithful, is the same. We are not responsible for our capacity, but we are responsible for the strategic investment of our time. When we have comparatively little to carry in the case it seems as full as when we have much because the less we have the more carelessly we pack it. The man who claims to have no time is most likely guilty of "careless packing." We never need more time than we have to do the whole will of God.

It could not be said of the late D. E. Hoste, General Director of the China Inland Mission, that his life was not extremely full, but he always made time for a deep and full prayer life. He gave that priority because he deemed it most important. But he did not arrive immediately at a mastery of his time. "It is easy to waste time," he wrote. "The missionary after breakfast may sit down to read the newspaper, or let time slip by in another way. But this cannot be done in business life. I have found the need of much watchfulness and self-discipline in this matter during my years in the interior. . . .

A sensitive conscience about the use of time needs to be maintained."

THREEFOLD PRESCRIPTION

Here are three constructive suggestions which may be of help to those who are seriously seeking to fill their lives with the greatest possible usefulness to God and yet to do it without undue strain and tension.

Stop leaks. Let us not consider our day only in terms of hours but in smaller areas of time. If we look after the minutes, the hours will look after themselves. Few men packed more into a lifetime than the late Dr. F. B. Meyer. Like John Wesley he divided his life into spaces of five minutes and chided himself if one of them passed in idleness. One would expect such a program to create intolerable strain, but not so with Dr. Meyer. According to his biographer: "His calm manner was not the sleep of an inactive mind, it was more like the sleep of a spinning top. He was never in a hurry because he was always in haste." Just a little while before his death he said to a friend, "I think I am an example of what the Lord can do with a man who concentrates on one thing at one time."

Perhaps few of us ordinary mortals can hope to achieve such a degree of concentration as to make every quarter hour carry the full quota of usefulness, but that does not excuse us from attempting it. For example, it is amazing how much reading can be squeezed into fragments of time redeemed from the trash pile. It is vain to wait until we get time to read seriously—we will never get it. We must make time to read by seizing the minutes we have. From the suggested analysis of our week, we should seek to detect unsuspected leakages of time, and with purpose of heart, *plug the leak.*

Study priorities. Much time which is not actually wasted is spent on things of only secondary importance. A fool has been described as a man who has missed the proportion of things. Some of us have the unfortunate tendency to be so engrossed in the secondary that we have no time left for the primary. We give such undue attention to petty details that matters of major importance are squeezed out. Especially is this so where spiritual things are concerned. Check on your analysis to see whether the spiritual is receiving adequate time or whether it is relegated to a secondary place by that which is good. Our Lord Himself indicated that the secret of progressive living was to sacrifice the pearl of inferior value for the pearl of transcendent worth. Are we doing the most important things or do we, because of the demands they make, procrastinate where they are concerned? Weigh carefully the respective values of the opportunities and responsibilities which claim attention. Omit altogether or give a very minor place to things of little importance. John Wesley used to say, "Never be unemployed, and never be triflingly employed." May I say here that *disciplined recreation and relaxation are not of secondary importance.* He who makes provision for the recovery of his physical and nervous powers is not triflingly employed. Jesus sat down at the well to relax in the midst of His busy ministry, and had He not done so He would have missed the Samaritan woman. He enjoyed ordinary social life and did not consider it waste of time to attend a wedding feast. We should from time to time review the analysis of our week to *see if we have our priorities right.*

Start planning. Without a proper plan we all tend to drift. If our life is a plan of God, there is appropriate work for each hour and the Lord will guide us as we pray and plan. Dr. John R. Mott used to devote half a day now and again to laying plans for the days ahead and he considered it time well invested. In the attitude of prayer ask, "How can I best plan today?" Divide it into parts. There are certain obvious obligations and duties, both spiritual and temporal, which naturally demand a place and adequate time should be allowed for these. Then there are secondary things which should be carefully pruned to a minimum and fitted in. When two duties pull in different directions, choose that which after prayer and thought seems more important. If a secular claim crowds a spiritual, do not concede the point unless you have good reason for doing so. In most lives there are every day short gaps left in the program which seem too short to fill with anything important, but these gaps must be filled. Why not write a letter? Don't wait until you get time to write—do it at once! Waiting until a more convenient time is the death knell of letter-writing. Allow sufficient time to insure punctuality, but not too much. Buy up the spare minutes as eagerly as a miser hoards his money. *Start planning your days.*

THE IMPELLING MOTIVE

To effect a radical change in our use of time will require strength of purpose and a real dependence on the Lord for His enabling. Not all of us possess inflexible wills but we may and should be "strengthened with might by his Spirit in the inner man." The use of time depends largely on the pressure of motive. Are there motives sufficiently compelling to enable us to change the pattern of our lives to run counter to long-indulged habits of laxity in the use of time? Henry Martyn found it impossible to waste an hour in his translation work, through the vision of nations waiting for the truth that lay locked up in the Book he was translating. The need of a lost world proved an impelling motive to redeem the hours. The driving force in the life of our Lord was revealed in one of His incidental sayings: "I do always those things that please him." Here are motives sufficiently potent to deliver us from wasting time which could be employed to bring Him glory and pleasure.

These considerations will act as a stimulus to some, but to others of a different disposition they may tend only to increase the problem and create deeper self-condemnation. While it is good to have a critical and sensitive conscience on this subject it is altogether bad to have what Paul called a "weak" conscience. A weak conscience requires instruction and discipline or it will exert a harmful tyranny. It is well to recognize that *after we have done all in our power there will still remain a vast area of need.* We cannot meet every call of need. If we sincerely before the Lord plan out our day along the lines suggested and carry it out to the best of our ability, we can and must leave it there. We should refuse to get into bondage about what has not been done. Circumstances beyond our control may prevent our carrying out a portion of our plan but that is no cause for self-accusation. Our responsibility is concerned only with the factors which lie within our power to control. If we feel harassed and the pressure on us becomes too great, the time has arrived to take stock of our commitments and to resolutely refuse more than we can discharge well and without undue strain. By thus simplifying our living we shall be able for more, and may confidently count on the Holy Spirit to guide us in a path in which we shall neither selfishly save our lives nor foolishly overspend our nervous and spiritual capital.

Such reorganization of living will demand stern self-discipline, but how well worth while. Even in this we are not left without Divine assistance: "For God gave us not a spirit of fearfulness: but of power and love and discipline" (II Tim. 1:7, A.S.V.). According to Dr. A. T. Robertson, the "spirit" here referred to is "the human spirit as endowed by the Holy Spirit," on whose co-operation we may count in this important matter.

18

WHAT CONSTITUTES A
MISSIONARY CALL?

As my Father hath sent me, even so send I you.
—John 20:21

OUR LIVES ARE OUR OWN TO SPEND, but we spend them only once. How important then, that we invest them wisely. Shall it be in the professional or business world? In the home ministry or the mission field? There are so many conflicting voices and such differing views on the subject of a missionary call that a decision is by no means easy to arrive at. But it is certainly possible to know the will of God.

The first essential in ascertaining this is the conviction that God does and will guide the sincere seeker. "I will instruct thee, and teach thee in the way which thou shalt go: I will guide thee with mine eye" (Ps. 32:8). With this promise beneath our feet we can confidently expect Him to unfold His perfect plan as we honestly seek to know it. Attitude of heart has an important bearing on the reception of guidance. If the object of our inquiry is to find the will of God in order to decide whether to do it or not, we may as well abandon our search.

God does not respond to such an attitude. But to the person who says, "Lord, only reveal Thy will to me and I will do it," there will be a certain answer.

BASIS OF CALL

A call to Christian work overseas has its basis in the command of the risen Lord which has come to be known as "The Great Commission." It is contained in a series of injunctions uttered between His resurrection and the day of His ascension and recorded in the first five books of the New Testament. In them, He lays on His disciples of all generations the responsibility of evangelizing the peoples of their own generation. The terms are clear and unequivocal. There are no geographical limitations, for they are to go into all the world. There is to be no racial discrimination, for their message is to all nations. There is to be no class privilege, for every creature must hear the emancipating news. In Christ there is to be no privilege of race or sex or class or culture.

In Matthew 28:18-20 the risen Lord commands them, relying on His almighty power, to make disciples of all nations and promises His presence until "the consummation of the age" (A.S.V.). In Mark 16:15 He individualizes the commission, commanding them to go "into all the world, and preach the gospel to every creature." In Luke 24: 47-49 He enforces the necessity of repentance and remission of sins being preached among all nations from Jerusalem as a starting point, but He specified that they were not to embark on their journey until they had been "endued with power from on high."

In John 20:21 He gives His commission in personal terms, lifting it to the level of His own commission: "As my Father hath sent me, even so send I you." The record in Acts 1:8 directs their thoughts away from national aggrandizement to the necessity of world-wide witness in the power of the Spirit. These five injunctions constitute the basis of a missionary call.

It is to be noted that our Lord was not giving advice but as sovereign Master He was issuing commands to His disciples. We may therefore assume that since He commanded this world-wide witness it is possible of achievement. If He is concerned with evangelism on a scale grand enough to reach every creature, He must have called sufficient in every generation to achieve the task—but many surely have failed to respond.

FEELING OR HEARING?

It is often said, "I do not feel a call to the mission field." But is a call felt or heard? Did Samuel hear the Lord's call or did he feel it when he responded: "Speak, Lord; for they servant heareth"? Did Isaiah hear or feel the voice of the Lord saying: "Whom shall I send, and who will go for us?" Did Paul hear or feel the call of the man of Macedonia, "Come over and help us"? Surely when we hear the Lord's call: "Go ye into all the world, and preach the gospel to every creature," it is a matter of obedience, not of feeling. The command is plain, however we feel about it. But when we hear and respond, we will soon experience a deepening feeling of concern, though the feeling is not the call. Feelings spring from the information of the mind and the attitude of the heart, and our lack of feeling may perhaps be attributable to an uninformed mind, an unsurrendered will, or a heart cold toward Christ.

To hear the general call of God to all His disciples to engage in world-wide witness is the first element in a call to a special sphere of service. We need no call other than the above Scriptures to lead us to recognize the general obligation resting on all believers. If we see a man drowning and we ourselves can swim, we do not need a special direction to make us go to his rescue. An inescapable obligation rests on us, and if we disregard it, we are guilty of the man's blood.

METHOD OF CALL

God's call does not come by any stereotyped method; it will vary with the individual. For this reason, while we can benefit from the experience of others, we should not expect to duplicate their guidance. There is infinite variety in all God's dealings with His children and He will adopt the method best suited to our own particular case.

For example, Philip was directed to work in Samaria because of fierce persecution. He was later led into the desert by an angel. Then he was directed by the Holy Spirit to join the Ethiopian treasurer in his chariot.

Paul was restrained by the Spirit from entering one field and constrained by the same Spirit to enter another. He experienced an inward "stop" in his spirit, and later an equally clear "release." But the final step which led to his missionary work in Rome was apparently not the result of any special revelation, but a combination of the exercise of his spiritual judgment and the inner witness of the Holy Spirit. God's method is variety, not uniformity.

His guidance will not be *mechanical*. The *"lucky dip"* method of handling Scripture which is sometimes adopted is not worthy of the God who created us rational beings. He speaks to our spirits by His Spirit, and very frequently through His Word. "His own sheep know his voice," Jesus said. When God speaks to us, we will know that He is speaking. Dr. K. D. Moynagh testified: "I have found that the voice of God has not been heard in the thunder—not in some sensational call from heaven; nor in the earthquake—some extraordinary experience or upheaval in the circumstances of my life. It has been in a still small voice —a voice of quiet stillness. God beckons us to come near to Him and then He speaks by the quiet unruffled inner stillness of His peace. This is the umpire in our decisions." "Faith accepts quiet guidance. Only unbelief demands a miracle."

What could be more reassuring than this promise of personal guidance from the Lord in time of crises? "Thine ears shall hear a word behind thee, saying, This is the way, walk ye in it, when ye shall turn to the right hand, and when ye turn to the left" (Isa. 30:21). God's method is distinctly personal.

Nor will His method be *visionary*. God deals with us in broad daylight. He can and occasionally does use a dream or vision as one factor in the indication of His will, but dreams or visions do not exempt us from the use of reason. It is worthy of note that even in Old Testament times a dream was repeated in different forms before it was accepted as a guide (Gen. 37:7-9; 41:3-7).

In the case of the vision which came to Paul (Acts 16:9), it should be noticed that he had already been called of God to misisonary work, had already completed one term of service and had already embarked on his second term. The vision constituted only one element in his guidance and was carefully safeguarded.

At the time it came to him he had already responded to the general obligation to take the Gospel to the unreached and was seeking the exact sphere of service. He was thus moving in line with the Word of God. When he experienced a restraint in his spirit, he immediately abandoned his own plans—God's set time for Asia and Bithynia had not yet arrived. He then stopped at Troas to wait for God to reveal the next step, and it was there he saw the vision. It is of passing interest to inquire how he knew it was a man of Macedonia, since they wore no distinctive dress. Is it unreasonable to suppose that Luke, himself a man from Macedonia, had been urging on Paul the pressing needs of his own land, and that he was the man of the vision?

Next Paul consulted his companions to check on his own judgment in the matter. Then having weighed up the various factors involved he came to his decision, "assuredly gathering" or "confidently inferring" that God had called them to preach the Gospel in Macedonia. The leading of his vision was thus in line with the Word of God, witnessed to by the Holy Spirit, for there was now no restraint on his spirit, confirmed by his companions and approved by his own judgment. Having arrived at his conclusion, even a hostile reception and a lacerated back did not shake this assurance.

God's method of call will always be *reasonable.* John Wesley said: "God generally guides me by presenting reasons to my mind for acting in a certain way." In other words, God generally guided him by the exercise of his sanctified judgment. It is true God sometimes gives extraordinary and spectacular guidance, but this is not the call, or even a necessary part of the call. Indeed, in most cases, such extraordinary confirmations usually come after the decision has been made and a step of faith taken, as in the case of Paul we have considered.

HOME OR OVERSEAS?

What are the relative claims of service at home or overseas? Cannot the Great Commission be fulfilled in either context? Indeed it can, and service overseas is not a higher form than service at home, if it is in the will of God. To find the will of God is the important thing. In considering this aspect, there are certain eliminating factors which may constitute guidance.

Consistently poor *health,* nervous disorders, the necessity to diet, a tendency to acute headaches or eyestrain or hereditary mental trouble would be an indication that in all probability the sphere of service would be in the homeland. If these conditions were present, it would be wise before proceeding further to get the opinion of a competent specialist.

Then there are *temperamental* conditions which would tend to disqualify for service overseas—an extremely hypersensitive or very highly strung nature, a tendency to melancholy or morbidity, an inseparable chum-complex, an inability to work with others, a nature which must manage everything and everybody.

If we are not *spiritually fruitful* in our present sphere of service, there is little point in our going overseas to be spiritually ineffective. The mere fact of engaging in full-time service overseas will not make us spiritually fruitful—the change is only geographical, not spiritual. We should earnestly seek God's face and comply with His conditions for fruitful service before contemplating overseas service.

It is often helpful to know the experience of godly and successful men who have met the same problem as faces us, and three quotations on the relative claims of the homeland and the foreign field follow.

Ion Keith-Falconer, of Arabia, expressed his conviction in these words:

> While vast continents still lie shrouded in almost utter darkness and hundreds of millions suffer the horrors of heathenism and Islam, the burden of proof rests on you to show that the circumstances in which God has placed you were meant to keep you out of the foreign mission field.

Reviewing his call to Mongolia, James Gilmour wrote:

> To me the question was not "Why go?"

Even on the low ground of common sense I seemed called to be a missionary. For is the kingdom not a harvest field? Then I thought it only reasonable to seek to work where the work was most abundant and the workers fewest. Laborers say they are overtaxed at home; what must be the case abroad, where there are wide-spreading plains already white to harvest with scarcely here and there a solitary reaper? My going forward is a matter of obedience to a plain command, and instead of seeking to assign a reason for going abroad, I would prefer to say that I have failed to discover any reason why I should stay at home.

In more recent times Bishop Stephen Neill, on returning to India for the third time said:

I place on record my conviction that the needs of the mission field are always far greater than the needs of the church at home, that no human qualifications, however high, render a man or woman more than adequate for missionary work, that there is no other career which affords such scope for enterprise and creative work, and that in comparison with the slight sacrifice demanded, the reward is great beyond all measure.

There appears to be no scriptural reason why we should expect a clearer call to service overseas than to service at home since the difference is only one of geography. We need no special call to apply to ourselves the general obligation on all believers to carry the Gospel into all the world. Rather should we expect a special call to exempt us from its requirements. Essentially, a call to foreign service does not differ from a call to service elsewhere.

But is this general obligation sufficient to warrant our engaging in foreign service without a specific and definite call? It is clear that Paul had such a call. "He is a chosen vessel unto me, to bear my name before the Gentiles . . . for I will show him how great things he must suffer for my name's sake" (Acts 9:15, 16). And again: "He said unto me, Depart: for I will send thee far hence unto the Gentiles" (Acts 22:21).

J. Hudson Taylor, out of a wide experience maintained:

> A missionary who is not clear on this point will at times be almost at the mercy of the great Enemy: when difficulties arise, when in danger or sickness, he will be tempted to raise the question which should have been settled before he left his native land: "Am I not in the wrong place?"

It has been said that facts are the finger of God, and certain facts concerning work in the homeland might be God's finger of guidance It is surely a reasonable presumption that if an area or community is adequately served with the Christian Gospel, the claims of that area should be secondary to those of an area inadequately served. This was one of the lessons taught by the Lord in the parable of the lost sheep and the ninety and nine safely in in the fold. It is an undeniable fact that the homelands are far more adequately served than the mission fields. In America there is one minister to every 535 people, for example, while in India there is one to 101,000, and in Southeast Asia there is one to 80,000. In the homelands, any seeking soul could, if he would, find the way to salvation. He could attend a church, listen on the radio, look at TV, buy a Bible or Gospel book, accost a Christian and inquire the way of life. On the mission field it is far different. Millions are doomed to live without hope and die without Christ because they are pagans by necessity. They could not hear the Gospel if they would, because there is no one to tell them. The missionary force is totally inadequate to meet the needs of areas yet untouched. These indisputable facts pondered over may prove to be the finger of God in guidance.

ASCERTAINING GOD'S WILL

This is often a painful and heart-searching experience, mainly because most of us have an inner reluctance to do the will of God without reservation. Even godly Henry Martyn knew the poignance of this struggle. "How much I have gone through during the last two or three years," he wrote, "to bring my mind to be willing to do the will of God when it should be revealed!" This is often the crucial point in guidance, and usually when it is safely past, the indication of the Divine will does not tarry.

In reaching a final decision concerning a missionary call the following practical suggestions may be helpful.

Purposefully commit your way to the Lord, confident that He will bring it to pass (Ps. 37:5). Since "without faith it is impossible to please him . . . he that cometh to God must believe that . . .

he is a rewarder of them that diligently seek him"
(Heb. 11:6), count upon the faithfulness of your
heavenly Father to convey His will to you.

Do not wait lethargically for something to happen, but give yourself to positive preparation. A
missionary on the eve of sailing recently testified
that some years earlier, although she did not then
have a missionary call, she purposely slanted her
training in that direction in case the Lord should
call her. And He did.

Gather all the authentic information you can of
mission fields, missionary societies, and types of
work. God cannot guide us with our heads empty
of the relevant facts. The call may come through
the reading of a book or magazine, seeing a pic-
ture, conversation with a missionary, an address,
or when we are alone in the place of prayer.

Squarely face the problems and difficulties of
missionary work and count the very real cost involved. When one gets down to the prosaic grind
of language study in a tropical climate in uncongenial conditions, any glamor attaching to overseas service quickly vanishes.

Consult two or three godly and well-informed
people in whose judgment you have confidence.
But do not allow them or even your own parents to
unduly influence you. It is your own life which is
involved, and the decision must be your own.

Obey every indication of the Divine will as it
becomes clear to you. Obedience to light given, results in the reception of further light.

When the time for final decision comes, carefully write out the pros and cons in two columns.
Trusting the Holy Spirit to guide your mental proc-

esses and to sway your will in the directions of the will of God, make your decision in the light of the information, advice, circumstances, light from the Scriptures, and the deepening inner conviction of the Holy Spirit. But do not act yet.

Subject your decision to the test of time. See if the conviction continues to deepen, and note whether the peace of God continues to pervade your heart. If so, conclude that the Lord is leading.

When Paul "assuredly gathered" that the Lord was calling to Macedonia, the record runs "immediately we endeavored to go." Do likewise, and God will show you the next step.

As you move forward you can expect further assurance from the Scriptures and confirmation from the surrounding circumstances. Extraordinary confirmations are not necessary, though they are sometimes given.

Having put your hand to the plow, resolutely refuse to turn back. Otherwise, our Lord says, you are "not fit for the kingdom of God." Never dig up in unbelief that which you have sown in faith. There is no need to review your guidance if you have acted in sincerity and in faith.

Beware of being sidetracked. The Adversary is likely to challenge your decision. Many have turned aside because of considerations of ambition or ease, and many more for reasons of matrimony or human affection. The Lord demands a supreme and overriding loyalty to Himself. "If any man come to me, and hate not his father, and mother, and wife, and children, and brethren, and sisters, yea, and his own life also, he cannot be my disciple.

. . . And whosoever doth not bear his cross, and come ofter me, cannot be my disciple . . . . So likewise, whosoever he be of you that forsaketh not all that he hath, he cannot be my disciple" (Luke 14:26, 27, 33).

19

SPIRITUAL MOUNTAINEERING

Give me this mountain.—Joshua 14:12

CALEB, the Mr. Greatheart of the Old Testament, was a man who never ceased growing. Passing years, instead of witnessing gradual eclipse, only served to increase his stature. He demonstrated the exhilarating truths that it is possible for the greatest achievement in life to take place in old age, and that there is no fixed retiring age in the Divine service. At every stage of life he merits our emulation; in no respect does he disappoint us. The open secret of his godly consistent, growing life is enshrined in five simple words which can be as true of us as they were of him: "He wholly followed the Lord."

CONSISTENT IN YOUTH

He appears on the stage of Israel's history as a comparatively young man. Nothing is recorded of his youth, but his subsequent record gives an accurate insight into his character as a young man. We are told nothing of the thirty years of our Lord's obscurity but the following three years of ministry tell us all we need to know of it. The crisis does not create but always reveals the man. Until the

185

crisis of shipwreck Paul was merely "one of certain prisoners," but he then became the undisputed master of the situation. The choice of Caleb, a ruler in Judah, as one of the twelve spies indicated the esteem in which he was held by leader and people.

Two qualities stand out conspicuously. First he showed *undaunted courage*. Moral courage is greater and rarer than physical courage but Caleb demonstrated both in the crisis at Kadesh. His moral courage shone out as he stood almost alone against the growing tide of popular opinion. This is one the most difficult tests for youth which craves popularity. It is difficult to pursue steadily an opposite course when "everyone is doing it." Not everyone is willing to sponsor a minority cause. It is all too easy to maintain a guilty silence in an adverse theological climate. It took no small degree of physical courage to persist in his attitude of faith when the stones began to fly, but he refused to be intimidated and bow to the wish of the majority.

Then his was a *robust and unwavering faith*, a quality which ranks high in the Divine scale of values. And his faith was the more remarkable because it flourished amid the miasmas of the unbelief rising from the majority report of the spies.

"The people be strong . . . the cities are walled, and very great . . . we saw the giants . . . we were in our own sight as grasshoppers . . . we be not able to go up against the people . . . they are stronger than we . . . a land that eateth up the inhabitants . . . all the people that we saw in it are men of a great stature" (Num. 13).

Into this chilling atmosphere of despair and unbelief, Caleb injects a shot of undaunted faith. "Let us go up at once and possess it; for we are well able to overcome . . . . The Lord . . . will bring us into this land . . . neither fear ye the people of the land; for they are bread for us . . . their defense is departed from them . . . the Lord is with us: fear them not" (Num. 13:30; 14:8, 9).

What a magnificent blending of faith and courage Caleb displayed! Were there fearsome giants? They were bread to them, and as one writer put it, "the bigger the giant, the bigger the loaf." Caleb and Joshua, the minority of faith, had seen all the ten had seen. Nor had they minimized the greatness of the task. The difference between them and the ten lay in the fact that while the ten had measured the strength of the giants against their own grasshopper strength, the two matched it against the omnipotence of God. Faith gives a true perspective. The ten urged, "Let us go back to Egypt." How soon they had forgotten the taskmaster's lash! But for Caleb there was no turning back. As we face our own particular giants and walled cities, are we emulating the ten or the two?

Unfrustrated in Mid-Life

Many who soared like rockets in youth have descended like sticks before the testings of middle life. True, these are not so volcanic as those of youth but they are much more subtle. Marriage knocks many a promising young person out of active spiritual warfare. Instead of transmuting the vanishing enthusiasms of youth into a worthy life purpose, we soften things and become anemic and insipid. There comes a loss of spiritual fervor, a

waning of personal devotion, the feeling that we
have now earned the right to ease up on self-denial
and to indulge ourselves a little, to yield to soften-
ing ease and settle down. Too often unrealized
ideals in marriage and home life come to be accepted as inevitable. With the fixing of life tend-
encies and habits, disillusionment, criticism, and
sometimes cynicism become the pattern of life in
greater or lesser degree. There comes an uncon-
scious deterioration of moral and spiritual fiber.

Caleb satisfactorily passed the test of youth but
how does he fare in the long drawn-out test of
middle life? His was a singularly hard and embit-
tering lot. Despite his own faith and courage he
was doomed to suffer a life of frustration and disappointment for forty years because of the unbelief of his contemporaries. Unbelief always affects
others, and infects them too, for it is very conta-
gious. Doomed to aimless wandering at the age
when his powers were at their zenith, he could
easily have become petulant and disgruntled. But
he successfully resisted the surrounding influences
and survived the long-sustained test without losing
moral or spiritual stature. He has soared with
wings as an eagle in his youth, and now he had
mastered the art of running without wearying,
stabilized by the vitality of his faith. But can he
walk without fainting?

TRIUMPHANT IN OLD AGE

Caleb provides us with a glorious conception of
the possibilities of old age. His supreme opportunity presented itself when he was eighty-five years
old. To him it was not "petering out" but pressing

on to new achievement; not descending the mountain but attacking a higher peak; not senility and sterility but adventure and achievement. His life moved steadily forward not to termination but to consummation. His last years were the best. He towers above his contemporaries at every age. In his youth he stood alone. In old age he climbs alone. After forty-five years of waiting for the fulfillment of the Divine promise he has lost none of his aggressive faith, none of his drive.

He was physically virile. "My strength is now, for war" (Josh. 14:11). Hear this man of eighty-five, who should have been putting on his soft slippers, talk about binding on shoes of iron so that he can ascend the mountain and rout the giants!

He was spiritually adventurous. "Give me this mountain" (14:12), he demanded. Which mountain? The one where dwelt the fearsome and invincible giants, of course. The mountain which more than forty-five years ago the unhurrying Lord had promised to Caleb and his seed. Still effervescent with youth he tackles his greatest task and achieves his greatest victory. His was not careless recklessness but calculating faith. He cherished a godly ambition and would be satisfied with nothing less than the complete fulfillment of the Divine promise.

"Give me this mountain" is a grand watchword for the aging Christian. Are we losing our spirit of aggression, becoming hesitant to risk a step of faith for God? Do we inwardly shrink from the rigors of the battle? Are we conscious of the fascination of things we left in our youth? Perhaps what we need is to remove our slippers, don the shoes of iron and ask the Lord for some forbidding mountain to conquer in His name. We can take courage from Caleb. The best lies yet ahead. Caleb never stopped growing because his faith never wavered.

Rev. C. H. Nash, who has trained a thousand young men and women for Christian service, retired from his principalship at the age of seventy, but not to rust out. At eighty he received assurance from the Lord of a further ten years of fruitful ministry, an assurance which was abundantly fulfilled. When he was nearing ninety I found him completing the reading of the sixth volume of Toynbee's monumental history, and after his ninetieth birthday I heard him lift a great congregation into the presence of God in a never-to-be forgotten prayer of dedication. Like Caleb he defied the natural order and continued increasing in stature into old age.

Perhaps the most noteworthy feature of Caleb's achievement was that of all the young men of Israel—all his own contemporaries had fallen in the wilderness—not one wholly expelled the enemy from his territory. But "Caleb drove thence the three sons of Anak," the record says. Concerning the others among whom Canaan was divided there runs the melancholy refrain: "They . . . did not utterly drive them out. . . . The Canaanites would dwell in the land. . . . There remaineth yet very much land to be possessed."

Two reasons were given for their failure to dispossess their enemies.

First, sheer *inability:* "They could not drive

them out." Their lack of faith resulted in lack of power.

Second, *indolence:* "How long will ye be slack to go and possess the land?" chided Joshua.

Why did the aged Caleb prevail where the youthful Israelites were frustrated? Here is his five-word secret: *he wholly followed the Lord.* The importance of this secret is emphasized by the number of times it is repeated in the record. Caleb with an approving conscience was able to assert it of himself: "I wholly followed the Lord" (Josh. 14:8). This was not boasting, but sober statement of fact. Moses, his revered leader who had every opportunity of appraising his character and attitude, asserted, "Thou hast wholly followed the Lord" (Josh. 14:9). But the most striking testimony comes from God Himself: "My servant Caleb . . . hath followed me fully" (Num. 14:24). Caleb completely dispossessed his enemies, giants and all, because he wholly followed the Lord. With him there were no divided loyalties. There was a steady obedience to light received and uncomplaining acceptance of the Divine will as he learned it; no murmuring at the unfairness of his lot. To him the will of God was good, acceptable, perfect. God moved very slowly, but he was content to wait God's time. In the language of the New Testament, as a logical act of worship he presented his body a living sacrifice to God, in striking contrast to the faithless multitude whose "carcases fell in the wilderness" because they were unwilling for that sacrifice.

Are there spiritual enemies in our lives which refuse to be dislodged, giants who laugh at our puny efforts to dispossess them? Do we find our charter much larger than the spiritual territory we actually occupy and enjoy? There is a reason. There are some areas in our lives in which we are not *wholly* following the Lord—some inner reservation, some flaw in dedication, something which short-circuits spiritual power and saps spiritual vitality. Caleb's open secret is for us too. Complete victory results from utter obedience.

> Make us Thy mountaineers;
> We would not linger on the lower slope;
> Fill us afresh with hope, Thou God of hope,
>   That undefeated, we may climb the hill
>   As seeing Him Who is invisible.
>   —AMY W. CARMICHAEL

Die climbing!

Moody Press, a ministry of the Moody Bible Institute, is designed for education, evangelization and edification. If we may assist you in knowing more about Christ and the Christian life, please write us without obligation to: Moody Press, c/o MLM, Chicago, Illinois 60610.